Class in China

Recent Titles in
Contributions in Political Science
Series Editor: Bernard K. Johnpoll

The Primordial Challenge: Ethnicity in the Contemporary World
John F. Stack, Jr., editor

Strangers or Friends: Principles for a New Alien Admission Policy
Mark Gibney

Intergovernmental Relations and Public Policy
J. Edwin Benton and David R. Morgan, editors

Breaking the Impasse in the War on Drugs
Steven Wisotsky

Citizen Participation in Public Decision Making
Jack DeSario and Stuart Langton, editors

Soviet Policy Toward East Germany Reconsidered
Ann L. Phillips

The Right to Life Movement and Third Party Politics
Robert J. Spitzer

Israel-Palestine: A Guerrilla Conflict in International Politics
Eliezer Ben-Rafael

Federal Lands Policy
Phillip O. Foss, editor

Begin's Foreign Policy, 1977–1983: Israel's Move to the Right
Ilan Peleg

Comparing Presidential Behavior: Carter, Reagan, and the Macho Presidential Style
John Orman

Toward a Theory of Eurocommunism: The Relationship of Eurocommunism to Eurosocialism
Armen Antonian

Power and Pluralism in American Cities: Researching the Urban Laboratory
Robert J. Waste

Class in China
STRATIFICATION IN A CLASSLESS SOCIETY

LARRY M. WORTZEL

CONTRIBUTIONS IN POLITICAL SCIENCE, NUMBER 168

GREENWOOD PRESS
NEW YORK · WESTPORT, CONNECTICUT · LONDON

Library of Congress Cataloging-in-Publication Data

Wortzel, Larry M.
Class in China.
(Contributions in political science, ISSN 0147-1066 ; no. 168)
Bibliography: p.
Includes index.
1. Social classes—China—History. 2. Social classes. 3. Social conflict—China. 4. Power (Social sciences) 5. Communism—China. 6. China—Economic conditions—1949- . I. Title. II. Series.
HN740.Z9S648 1987 305.5′0951 86-29394
ISBN 0-313-25498-2

Library of Congress Catalog Card Number: 86-29394
ISBN: 0-313-25498-2
ISSN: 0147-1066

First published in 1987

Greenwood Press, Inc.
88 Post Road West, Westport, Connecticut 06881

Printed in the United States of America

The paper used in this book complies with the Permanent Paper Standard issued by the National Information Standards Organization (Z39.48-1984).

10 9 8 7 6 5 4 3 2 1

Contents

Tables and Figures

TABLES

FIGURES

Preface

This book began as a means to satisfy intellectual interest in the concept of class sparked by the events in Poland revolving around the Solidarity movement. The study was further stimulated by issues raised by the Socialist Democracy movement in China, especially by the arrest of Wang Xizhe in Guangzhou. The more I read on the subject, the more I began to question the viability of the Marxian concept of class as an ordering concept for stratification in contemporary socialist society, particularly with respect to China.

As a socialist state governed by a Marxist-Leninist party, the People's Republic of China (PRC) claims to have eliminated the antagonistic class relations that, according to the Marxist interpretation of social reality, exist under capitalism. Officially in the PRC there are classes, but they no longer have antagonistic interests. The state form is a dictatorship of the proleteriat that has as its primary stated goal the interests of the workers. The questions that occurred were not easily answered by a reading of the official statements concerning class made by the Chinese Communist Party (CCP). If the antagonistic interests of classes were eliminated, why did members of the Socialist Democracy Movement claim that the Party had elevated itself to the status of a new ruling class? What other voices in China had sounded complaints about the equity of the distribution of wealth and political power under this dictatorship of the proletariat? How did one gain access to allocative power?

I suggested as a working hypothesis to guide the inquiry that the nature of political and economic power in China still has a class content (in the Marxian sense); that class relations are still, and may continue to be, antagonistic; and that instead of being a dictatorship of the proletariat, the CCP has evolved into a new ruling class that has its own interests.

Such a proposal was not new to Marxist political philosophy. Similar suggestions are in the tradition of Leon Trotsky, Georgy Lukacs, Antonio Gramsci, Herbert Marcuse, Milovan Djilas, and Rudolf Bahro, to name but a few Marxist thinkers. Indeed, Mao Zedong and the ill-fated "Gang of Four" made similar suggestions.

My interests in the general field of epistemology and interpretive understanding led to a deeper investigation—not simply into the structure of class in China but into the history of the term, its "archaeology," to borrow a concept from Foucault. Thus what began as a relatively straightforward review of literature developed into a hermeneutical exercise to analyze the Marxian concept of class and to critically apply the concept to stratification in China today.

To date there has been no thoroughgoing analysis of classes in socialist China. Treatment of the composition of socialist societies has been either from the perspective of the accepted definition of class as interpreted by the ruling party or an exercise in "exegesiology," a discourse with the Communist Party interpretation by those who would claim to have better understood Marx's works than the Party itself. This book attempts an analysis of a class society under existing socialism. It combines an interpretive analysis of the texts of Marxism and Maoism with a critique—internal to Marxist epistemology as well as transcendent and external to it—of the epistemological underpinnings of the concept of class in China. By applying interpretive approaches from critical theory to analysis of contemporary literature in China, I ask: Who makes the rules about which class is the owner of the means of production, and are these rules accepted by the society as a whole? How does legal ownership of the means of production relate to functional control of production, consumption, compulsion, and administration?

At the same time that this book analyzes China, it is also a more general analysis of social stratification under state socialism. At the general theoretical level it has implications for tendencies inherent in the structure of socialist political reality. It suggests that orthodox Marxism, as a critique of political interest in capitalist society, lacks the analytical tools for a similar critique of the Marxist-Leninist state.

More significantly, the results of the inquiry suggest that the communist doctrine of democratic centralism has degraded the importance of the concept of class as a means to explore political interest in communist states.

ACKNOWLEDGMENTS

I would like to pay special thanks to my wife, Tina, and my sons, Kerry and Leonard, for their tolerance. Much of the time devoted to this book was taken from them. Leonard deserves separate mention for his help in preparing the final manuscript. While I acknowledge full responsibility for the work and any errors it may contain, many people have been generous with their time in reviewing the manuscript. Foremost are Professors Ben Kerkvliet, Manfred Henningsen, Sen-dou Chang, Yas Kuroda, and Oliver Lee of the University of Hawaii-Manoa, whose counsel has been invaluable. I also want to thank Mr. Ewald Cheer, and other faculty members of the Chinese Department, U.S. Defense Language Institute, for giving me the lessons of ''political reeducation'' at the hands of the CCP.

The following institutions allowed me access to their collections: the East Asia Collection, Hoover Institution on War, Revolution, and Peace; the China collection at the National University of Singapore; and the Universities Service Center, Hong Kong.

Abbreviations

BR	*Beijing Review*
CCP	Chinese Communist Party
CR	Cultural Revolution
FBIS	Foreign Broadcast Information Service
FEER	*Far Eastern Economic Review*
GMRB	*Guangming Ribao*
HQ	*Hong Qi*
JFJB	*Jiefang Junbao*
JFRB	*Jiefang Ribao*
JJNJ	*Jingji Nianjian*
JPRS	*Joint Publications Research Service*
PLA	People's Liberation Army
RMRB	*Renmin Ribao*
RMWX	*Renmin Wenxue*
SW	*Selected Works of Mao Zedong*
WXPL	*Wenxue Pinglun*

Class in China

1

Introduction

In China, one-quarter of the world's population—a billion people—live in a society that takes Marxism-Leninism and Mao Zedong thought as its guide. After the victory of the Communist Party in the 1949 revolution, another revolution, the Cultural Revolution, occurred there. Both of these upheavals were based on interpretations of Marx's theory of class. This book asks two fundamental questions about Marxist class theory: How valid is the theory in a state where most of the means of production are no longer privately owned? Is there a better explanation than orthodox Marxist class theory for social stratification in socialist China?

MARXISM AND SOCIAL CLASS

Marx's works and the majority of Marxist research and thought today deal with the questions of capitalist production and the nature of the capitalist state. According to Marx's critique, under capitalism the political party system, the state and its administrative agencies, law, access to education—even the content of that education—are conditioned (some would even say determined) by the class structure. Those who own the means of production (land, machinery, tools, draft animals, labor, and factories) wield the power in a society. They use their power to ensure that the institutions of that society (law, the administrative bureaucracy, the arts, and literature) work to their advantage.

This critique of capitalist society—the Marxian interpretation of the relations among property, capital, and the ownership of the means of production—is the point of departure for this book. Rather than dwell on the analysis of class in capitalist societies, this study uses the People's Republic of China (PRC) to investigate (1) what happens to political institutions and social relationships when the means of production are publicly owned; (2) how an interpretive analysis of stratification in socialist China can help to provide a conceptual framework to understand the articulation of political interest in socialist states; (3) whether the Marxian concept of class is a viable way to understand stratification, interest articulation, and political reality after the means of production are socialized; and (4) the validity of assertions that the Communist Party becomes a "new class."

There has been insufficient thought devoted to such questions among those who study the phenomenon of social stratification in socialist societies.[1] However, as did events in Hungary in 1956 and Czechoslovakia in 1968, the events in Poland concerning the Solidarity movement force us to ask whether a communist party genuinely represents the interests of workers or, instead, its own interests.

Milovan Djilas has suggested that a ruling communist party in a socialist society becomes a "new class with its own interests that are antagonistic to the interests of workers and the mass of the state's citizens."[2] Notwithstanding Djilas's comments, the Chinese Communist Party claims to have eliminated antagonistic class relations by ensuring that the form of state power, a dictatorship of the proletariat, looks after the interests of the workers. However, if the antagonistic interests of classes were eliminated, why did members of China's Socialist Democracy Movement, in 1978–1979, claim that the CCP had elevated itself to a new ruling class? What other voices in China had sounded complaints about the equity of the distribution of wealth and political power under this dictatorship of the proletariat?

In China, as in Eastern Europe, suggestions that the Communist Party has not been acting in the interests of workers and peasants have been accompanied by calls for reform. Chinese dissidents—Marxist and non-Marxist—charge that the CCP seeks only to pursue its own interests.[3] Meanwhile, the commune system in China continues to undergo a transformation that, on the surface, belies the original goals of collectivization as a step toward communism.[4] In the face of such fundamental problems within the socialist camp, an attempt at a new analysis of political power in socialist society seems prudent.[5]

Marxist parties have largely defined themselves out of the problem of producing a theory of class that, at the same time, is a critique of the socialist state. One way they have done so is by defining class as a direct function of private ownership of the means of production; then, through claims that such private ownership has been eliminated, antagonistic classes are said to have been eliminated. A second way they have done so is by presenting the classical texts of Marxism (the works of Marx, Engels, and Lenin) as historically revealed truth. Treated as a legitimating authority, these texts have become canonized; attempts to use them critically have been blocked.

Hermeneutics and Political Analysis

Marx, Engels, and Lenin wrote in specific historical periods, addressing the problems and phenomena of the respective period. Their texts must be read as a discourse with their fellows—a personal dialogue about social conditions in their world. However, conditions have changed since the texts were written. If they are to be understood today, they must be taken as a paradigm for a method that involves the comprehension and critical explanation of the contemporary world.[6] A dogmatic and fundamental reliance on the original texts elevates them to the sacred. They are memorized, worshipped and enshrined, but not used critically.

When the texts of Marxism (or any other texts) are treated as sacred, as representing the one true insight into truth or science, they become reified. The texts are transformed into dogma, with the Communist Party represented as the sole instrument of authentic interpretation. The movement by the Party toward canonization necessitates reliance on a science of interpretation, or hermeneutics, as the primary method employed in a contemporary study.[7] Such an approach cuts through the text to engage it in a critical dialogue intended to uncover double meanings, symbol, and analogy.[8] This hermeneutical method, in practice, is a theory of rules that preside over the conduct of an interpretation.[9] In this study by text, we must understand more than the literary model. Here the concept of text also includes speech, ritual, and symbol.[10] Paul Riceour's work is particularly instructive in this regard. Riceour tells us that "this notion of text—thus freed from the notion of writing—is of considerable interest. Freud often makes use of it, particularly when he compares the work of analysis to translating from one language to another; the dream account is an unintelligible text for which the analyst substitutes a more intelligible text.''[11]

Unlike the approach taken when a positivist methodology is adopted, there is no ''methods'' text readily available to instruct in the hermeneutical approach.[12] An interpretation cannot pass mathematical or statistical tests of truth or falsehood. An interpretation follows rules; it strives toward truth through a test in written or oral discourse. An interpretation must accurately reflect reality, but quantitative procedures may not verify the conceptual categories undergoing analysis—in the case of this book, the concept of class. Instead, the truth of the interpretation is verified ''in a dialogue between concept and evidence, conducted by successive hypotheses, on the one hand, and empirical research, on the other.''[13] At the same time, an interpretation is not a value-free exposition of a body of research or data. Any interpretation is ''inherently colored and partly conditioned by the social (mental and cultural) paraphernalia that we carry with us from the past into the present.''[14] Hermeneutics, as a science of interpretation, is a rigorous application of an analytical method in search of truth. It aims at a series of dialogues in which the interpretor must be concious of his or her own subjectivity and must avoid projecting that subjectivity into the interpretation.[15]

The goal of this study is to draw the reader, regardless of his or her ideological viewpoint, into a dialogue both with the texts that are examined and with the study itself. Ultimately this should engender a critique of the Marxian concept of class, a concept that is at the heart of the utopia offered by the Communist Party to the Chinese people.

Those who treat Marxism as a body of dogma, as ''revealed truth,'' will be able to dismiss this interpretation as ''revisionist.''[16] The reader should keep in mind that the object of this book is a critical examination of social stratification in China in an attempt to derive a theory that accounts for political relations there. Within this context the book advances tentative hypotheses about the nature of social stratification, hence political power, that have application for other socialist states.[17]

Using China as an example but also drawing on sources from Eastern Europe and the USSR, the book demonstrates that in many cases the manner in which property is owned may not be the primary consideration on which to judge the existence or nonexistence of a ''class society.'' Instead, the very question of what definition of ownership that a state—or a ruling group—chooses to problematize sets the conditions for interpretation of any data collected.[18] The way the questions are posed (and the interests of those posing the questions) masks the existence of social stratification and may also limit opportunities for political expression. Whoever is placed in the epistemologically privileged position of the subject of an inquiry (the party, the "people," or a sector of the population) dictates what political relationships become relevant in the society.

This interpretation considers ideas from theorists concerned with the analysis of language—its social and political implications. Language is culture-bound and is symbolically relevant for different groups, at different times, with different meanings. Moreover, these meanings are "layered"; they are based on substrata of meaning inherited in a particular linguistic tradition.[19] With regard to China, we must attempt to understand the term "class" from three cultural perspectives: its use in the Marxist-Leninist vernacular; its development and use in traditional society; and its use in the Maoist epistemology. To assist in reaching this understanding, the book brings to bear relevant critiques of class theory in socialist states from the Yugoslav Praxis Group, Milovan Djilas, Rudolf Bahro, and others.[20]

"Social Paraphernalia"

Can an American who views society and the state as outcomes of the actions of individuals who, through discourse, engage in politics render an unbiased study on China?[21] Is it possible for a person who believes that a society is best governed through pluralism (where people, and subcultures, associate in the shared agreement that they will disagree about beliefs, values, and the jurisdiction of government) to fairly evaluate political associations in a socialist state? These are questions that both the author and the reader should ask if bias is to be avoided.

Analysis of the nature of politics in contemporary Chinese society need not demand a belief in Marx's millennial vision. However, such an analysis, if it is to reduce the bias inherent in a non-Marxist, requires one to struggle to avoid, on the one hand, making an ideological attack on political society in China; on the other hand, one should avoid idealizing Maoist egalitarianism. Remaining conscious of one's "intellectual baggage" will assist in this analysis.

SOURCES AND LIMITATIONS

Travel and research in the PRC are rigidly controlled by the Chinese government and are overseen by CCP organs through the network of Party units. Consider what happened to Lisa Wischer, the graduate student who was held for doing economic research and whose materials were seized and, more recently, to John Burns, the *New York Times* reporter held for espionage because he went into an area denied to foreigners by Beijing. The primary limitations on research, discussed in more detail in a later chapter, were imposed by the rigid control over ideas in China. The system of neighborhood Party committees and enterprise Party committees exercises a chilling form of informal surveillance over interpersonal contacts among persons, particularly foreigners and native Chinese citizens, through an omnipresent watchfulness.[22] The existence of a large volume of internally restricted (*nei bu*) books and information in libraries also severely limits the amount and quality of contemporary political material to which the researcher has access. Moreover, a request by the author to conduct independent survey research or sponsored field research on attitudes toward class was rejected by a senior official of the Chinese Academy of Social Sciences.[23]

Still, the sources available—newspapers and periodicals, popular literature, school texts, and some personal interviews—were more than adequate for this study. Although it would have been preferable to remain some length of time in each place the author visited to conduct survey research, extensive travel in China and informal interviews complemented the author's readings and research. Admittedly, excellent research has been done on Chinese political elites. This is important because the Party is an elite group; but the interpretation presented herein is unique to scholarship on China.

Scalapino, for instance, has studied the composition and recruitment of elites in some detail.[24] But his studies avoid a broad analysis of class and concentrate only on the elite structure. Whereas Scalapino admits that his work, and elite studies in general, may not advance to the level of general theory, this study seeks to address that level of theory.[25] Lucian Pye analyzes the Chinese political system from a different viewpoint—the formation of political factions in China.[26] But he disregards (economic) sectoral considerations and does not attempt to relate political power to the functional control of the means of production, a topic considered by Parris Chang.[27] Richard Kraus, who presents a thorough analysis of class *conflict* in China, never analyzes the *concept* of class. He accepts the Party's interpretation uncritically, as an a priori concept.[28]

This book reviews theories of class in an attempt to identify bases of social stratification under socialism. The work takes the nature of the politico-economic system as its object of analysis and views the system from the perspective of various social groups. Included in the book are analyses of the Chinese Communist Party epistemology and the official position of the Party on the existence of classes in socialist states; reflections of class society in popular Chinese contemporary literature; a critique of Party abuse of privilege; and an analysis of social stratification in contemporary China. The book concludes with proposals for a new way to understand social stratification and the articulation of political interest in socialist China.

2

Class in China: The Traditional View

Marxism came to China in 1919, less than a century ago. The Chinese Communist Party was formed in 1921. Before that time, for over twenty centuries, China enjoyed a relatively stable political tradition. This chapter explores how the political order was conceptualized in traditional Chinese thought, for the traditional conception of order affected the conception of class in Marxist China.

Etienne Balasz describes China as a "permanently bureaucratic society."[1] He points out that for the expanse of Chinese history, despite numerous changes in dynastic succession, there was an "uninterrupted continuity of a ruling class of scholar-officials."[2] Through the centuries although individuals were in politically precarious positions, rotated or forced out of officialdom, the society was administered by this bureaucratic elite of scholar-officials. This bureaucratic elite drew its strength from the indispensable social function it performed.[3]

The bureaucratic elite administered China, acting as the government, but it did not comprise the ruling class of Chinese society. The administrators for the most part were still commoners, governed by a "divine" nobility who rose to rule by ascription. As early as the Shang Dynasty (1751–1111 B.C.) and into the Spring and Autumn Period (770–476 B.C.), Chinese nobles traced their origins to descent from a god or deified ancestor.[4]

Donald J. Munro illustrates this point with this quote: "The Shang house, for example, was founded by a person who hatched from a swallow's egg at the command of a deity; and Prince Millett, the founder of the royal Zhou family, came into the world after his mother walked on a toeprint made by the lord on high."[5] The reader should bear in mind, however, that there was not an unbroken dynastic line in China. Dynastic lines were not necessarily transmitted by bloodline. Rather, there was a succession of dynasties changing as a result of prowess in war, ability, or merit.[6] The hereditary principle of nobility nonetheless operated through a series of aristocratic families in each dynasty.[7]

The object of this historical overview is to enable the reader to understand the unique historico-cultural basis of Chinese social distinctions. The rules that define class in China today are part of a field of meaning that cannot be restricted to the concept of class post-Marx. There has been a layering of meaning onto the original understanding of the term "class" that, although based on a continuity with established understanding and social practice, has changed the meaning of the term to conform to new socioeconomic and political relations.[8] Older terms, employed in earlier times, remain the same in the language, using the same ideographs, but the philosophical concepts involving these terms have "evolved and changed their meanings" over the years.[9]

To understand the field of meaning that refers to the Marxian term "class," one must understand four underlying assumptions about social stratification in China on which the concept depends: (1) the nature of Chinese philosophical thought, which stresses the strict classification of things according to their correct name and function; (2) a sometimes implied but more often stated imperative requiring people to act in a manner befitting their station in life and structural position in the family; (3) an epistemological position, taken from the thought of Mao Zedong but with a basis in traditional Chinese philosophy, that is dependent upon a dialectical analysis of phenomena; and (4) Marxist class analysis, which relates people to the means of production. This chapter discusses the first two assumptions; chapter 3 discusses the third and fourth assumptions.

MYTHS AND CLASS

For the reader who has been educated in the West, it may be helpful first to make some comparisons between Western and Chinese philosophical traditions. In Plato's *The Republic*, Socrates proposed telling the inhabitants of the city that although they are all brothers,

> while God moulded you, he mingled gold in the generation of some, and those are the ones fit to rule, who are therefore the most precious; he mingled silver in the assistants [the second class of guardians]; and iron and brass in farmers and the other craftsmen. Then, because of being all akin you would beget your likes for the most part, but sometimes a silver child may be born from a golden or a golden from a silvern, and so with all the rest breeding amongst each other. The rulers are commanded by God first and foremost that they be good guardians of no person so much as of their own children, and to watch nothing else so carefully as which of these things is mingled in their souls. If any child of theirs has a touch of brass or iron, they will not be merciful to him on any account, but they will give him the proper value to his nature, and push him away among the craftsmen and farmers; if again one of them has the gold or silver in his nature, they will honor him and lift him among the guardians or assistants, since there is an oracle that the city will be destroyed when the brass or the iron shall guard it.[10]

The gold, silver, and brass or iron proposed by Plato are metaphors for the hierarchy of reason, spirit, and the baser appetites in human behavior.[11] For the society in *The Republic* they represent an aristocracy of merit that, as in Confucian society, cannot be passed along by ascription.

The Platonic view of society was both social commentary and normative political philosophy. As social commentary it addressed what Plato saw as the dissolution of the social order around him. As normative theory it proposed a system to organize and manage the affairs of a community—public affairs—in pursuit of "the good life." Central to attaining this good life was the selection and development of people who, using the capacity to reason, could settle on mutually acceptable conditions for community life through dialogue. Struggle for competitive advantage and contention for power were wrong; the good life was to be attained through discourse.

Early Chinese mythology also bases the right to govern on the ability to reason, establishing an aristocracy of merit. The archetypal sage-king Yao established a government system, borders, and a means to order society.[12] Yao is said to have reigned in the years 2357–2255 B.C. Yao was replaced by Shun, who was the wisest of Yao's ministers. Shun's reign is said to have been 2255–2205 B.C. For both of these rulers the path to royalty was through virtue, wisdom, and merit.

Shun, according to legend, was followed by Yu, who is credited with taming the waters of a great flood by creating a system of dams and canals.[13] Interestingly, Shun is said to have banished his own son from the kingdom so that no relative would be favored for elevation of sovereignty. Yu, however, was succeeded by his own son, establishing the Xia (Hsia) dynasty and a tradition of royalty.[14]

A ruler's function during those times was to coordinate "the three great forces in the ancient Chinese chronology: the heavenly, the earthly, and the human."[15] The government was established to organize the nation, protect it, feed it, ensure water conservancy, regulate currency, and educate the populace. Ultimately the emperor was blamed for even meteorological catastrophes.

In the Platonic myth humankind is formed of elements of different values, a metaphor both for the natural differences that occur among people and for the worth that these differences have for society as a whole. Offspring do not necessarily have the same qualities as their parents but must be treated in accordance with their innate nature. In the Chinese mythological texts leaders were originally selected for their innate nature, but by the Xia dynasty the throne was passed on by ascription.

In the Platonic myth any person may be born with the good qualities of the metals of value; any child can become a guardian, a philosopher-king. In China a similar system gave way to a succession of dynasties in which there were two classes of people on the earth; the noble ruler and the rest of the populace, including government officials, who were merely royal subjects. Only later, in the sixth century B.C., through the Confucian *Analects*, does there come into wide practice a philosophical system in China that criticizes dynastic rule and acknowledges that persons of low birth may have qualities that are exceptional.[16] Confucius recognized that persons of noble birth, although they may inherit important positions, are not necessarily capable of ruling effectively. Therefore, in his philosophical system emphasis is placed on merit and performance as measured against standardized objective criteria. Those males who performed well in classical studies and could demonstrate the quality of their scholarship were fit to administer the state. These people were to be the scholar-officials who controlled the functions of the state in the bureaucracy. The emperor was conceived ideally as an intelligent, able, and uniquely ethical person.[17]

THE INFLUENCE OF LANGUAGE

Normative political theory does not often develop as a reflection of practice in a given age or time. Rather, at the time political theories are developed, they *contend* with and criticize the dominant views. Normative theories talk about how things *ought* to be. Such is the case with the dominant political philosophy in China. Yao, Shun, and Yu were idealized as sage-kings; but after them, as emperors rose to the throne by ascription, political thought concentrated on the idealized re-creation of these men. For the Greeks, the sense of the political and the concept of governance were tied to the *polis* (the city-state) and discourse over human social relations in the polis. For the Chinese, the sense of the political was (and is now) tied to a patriarchal sense of correct rule, or governance. The traditional Chinese view of political life deals with the governance of man and the management of government affairs; not with discourse over the good life.

Good governance, in the Confucian view, implied right behavior (both ethical and correct) by the ruler, the government official, and the subject—behavior according to one's rank and position.

These concepts are apparent in the very structure of the ideograph meaning government (*zheng zhi*). The term *zheng* implies appropriateness, correctness, and execution of rule or law, righteousness, and justice. *Zheng* relates to politics, administration, or governance, but always with the implication that government must be ethical and correct. The ideograph *zhi* implies control, management, punishment, and, in addition, a seat of government. Its root implies involvement with the governance and management of water. In fact, that is the thesis of Karl Wittfogel's book *Oriental Despotism*. The management of water is also the basis for the rule of Yu.

At the heart of the question concerning who should rule in China and how those who rule should behave is a tendency to prescribe very circumscribed roles to persons and things: a tendency that has a basis in language. In Chinese society, particularly in classical Confucianism, standard or ritualized behavior is perceived to be the proper expression of human social behavior. People are assumed to be willing to accept the social obligations required by the position they occupy in the social structure.[18]

All societies observe conventions of behavior and have a social structure. But the very structure of the Chinese language, to an extent much greater than in the English language, is based upon categorization or, if you will, classification. Because of this structural characteristic people and things are often placed into immutable categories that describe not only their function but their behavior.[19] To a certain extent this is true of any language, for language is a set of shared meanings. But in the Chinese language there is great concentration on the written form of a word, and when one understands how an ideograph is formed, one has a key to both its pronunciation and the general class or category of things to which it belongs.[20]

Each ideograph contains a radical, which provides a clue to its meaning, and a phonetic, which is a symbol for its general sound. For example, the radical *shui*, represented by three dots, or drops, means water. Every ideograph that contains this radical is generally related to things in the liquid state. The radical *niao*, which looks like a sideview of a fowl, means bird. The names of all fowl contain this ideograph. Because of this tendency to assign everything a classifier, individuals and things are known and recognized only as members of a class or category of things.[21] In fact, entire categories of nouns have their own measure words, which are words that function as classifiers. The nouns cannot be used in written or oral communication without these classifiers. Persons of ordinary birth or position are counted using the classifier *ge*; high officials and respected persons are counted using the classifier *wei*; sticks, arrows, branches, fingers, and other long things use the classifier *zhi*; and so on.

Not only are people and things classified by their function or state of being, but specific forms of behavior are ascribed to certain categories. The process of naming things in the world circumscribed the roles and uses to which people and things could be put. Accordingly, Confucius is to have told an interlocutor:

> What is necessary is to rectify names. . . . If names be not correct, language is not in accordance with the truth of things. If language be not in accordance with the truth of things, affairs cannot be carried on to success. When affairs cannot be carried on to success, proprieties and music will not flourish. When proprieties and music do not flourish, punishments will not be properly awarded. When punishments are not properly awarded, the people do not know how to move hand or foot. Therefore, a superior man considers it necessary that the names he uses may be spoken appropriately, and also that what he speaks may

be carried out appropriately. What the superior man requires, is just that in his words there may be nothing incorrect.[22]

This insistence upon the correctness of name and function is characteristic of Chinese philosophy from ancient times to modern. Confucianism assumes that people learn by imitating models.[23] The cultured person and the less cultured alike are assumed to consciously seek virtuous models for emulation.[24] In the context of modern times this insistence upon the correctness of name, position, and behavior is mirrored in the Communist Party rectification campaigns that have been carried out since the middle of the anti-Japanese War.[25] These campaigns ensure that social being remains consistent with its model in Marxist-Leninist-Mao Zedong thought. In ancient times, after Confucius entire schools of thinkers developed theories of names. The philosopher Gong-sun Long, in his famous essay on the distinction between a white horse and a horse, carried this rectification to an extreme, insisting that the connotation of a white horse, and its nature, are so radically different from that of a black or brown horse that a white horse is more than simply a horse. If one needs a white horse, no other kind of horse will satisfy this need. Thus Gong-sun Long concludes that a white horse is not a horse.[26]

Hsun-tsu, like Gong-sun Long, insists that once names are confused, the distinctions between superior, important men and inferior or subservient men will disappear. The scholars, who form a class of persons who guard the laws of meaning in the classical texts, must be clear that standards are used in the regulation of names. Otherwise the distinctions between the eminent and the humble will disappear:

> [If there are no fixed names,] but men begin to discriminate the different forms of things on the basis of their own particular observations, each applying his own names and interpreting the phenomena in his own fashion, then the relationships between names and realities will become obscured and entangled, the distinction between humble and eminent will become unclear, and men will no longer discriminate properly between things that are the same and those that are different.[27]

TRADITIONAL CLASS DISTINCTIONS

It is from this basis that the traditional social distinctions in China emerged. The noble were touched by the dieties forming a ruling class;

all other classes were subdivisions of commoners, held in descending order of esteem.[28] The scholar-officials—state bureaucrats, court administrators, and officers of the military forces—were able to act as the guardians of the laws of meaning, *shi* or *shidafu*. These people were the ruling gentry. According to Ping-ti Ho, there were three strata of scholar-officials: in the first stratum, ranks 1 through 3 of officialdom had great power; they could recommend their subordinate officials for rank and their descendants could inherit their positions. In the second stratum ranks 4 through 7 were heads of junior central courts and bureaus, censors, county magistrates, and prefects. They could neither recommend subordinates for office nor transmit hereditary privilege. Like the middle stratum, ranks 8 and 9 of the bureaucracy could not recommend people for office or pass along their position hereditarily. Officials of this lowest stratum filled positions as assistant and deputy magistrates, submagistrates, and public safety officials at the county level.[29]

The next rung on the social ladder below the scholar-officials was occupied by the peasant, the group that provides sustenance to the kingdom. Ranked below the peasants were artisans or craftsmen, who make the necessities for life. The lowest strata were businessmen, tradespeople, and the ordinary soldiers of the military.[30] By the time of the Northern Sung dynasty (A.D. 960–1127) the position of the military had so deteriorated that beggars and vagrants were being recruited into it, branded on the face and hands to prevent their escape, and led by eunuchs.[31]

The question of whether these groups in traditional social stratification were classes is contentious. For Marxists, China's history is divided into periods—slave, feudal, and (from the Opium Wars until the Communist Revolution) semifeudal/semicolonial—which were characterized by different forms of ownership of the means of production.[32] There is a tendency to ascribe the characteristics of castes to these social groupings in China. Balasz, for example, asks whether the "uninterrupted continuity of a ruling class of scholar-officials" was an estate, a class, or a caste.[33] Individually, he says, scholar-officials were in very precarious positions; although the functional positions remained unchanged, persons were routinely forced in and out of positions.[34] Balasz concludes, however, that they were a class because of "their economic basis (salaries and ownership of land), their uniform style of life, and their traditionalist outlook."[35] Wolfram

Eberhard also calls the gentry (scholar-official, or *shi*) a ruling class but notes that they were not an aristocracy or nobility.[36]

Ping-ti Ho disagrees with this characterization. He does not believe that the four functional orders in Chinese societies formed classes; rather, he sees them as members of a single class—the commoner as opposed to the noble.[37] However, Ho was not sufficiently differentiated the term "class" from caste. These groups formed classes in that their members' lives were characterized by group consciousness, their social relations and life-styles were similar, and their economic bases, as Balasz points out, were similar.[38] Ownership of the means of production, however, was a clouded issue. The manual-mental division of labor was probably the most important single point of social stratification in traditional Chinese society. Talented people, according to the Confucian ethic, performed mental labor; but there was still a hierarchy of skilled manual labor.[39] Compounding the difficulty of differentiating the nature of stratification, once mercantile capitalism developed in the sixth century A.D., it became possible to buy positions in the bureaucracy and to acquire what was once inherited land, creating an incongruity between status and class position. Merchants, who were held in disregard, often controlled wealth and property and had strong links to both officials and nobles.[40] Even allowing the distinction between ruler and ruled, it is fair to address these four functional groups of commoners as classes. Surely they were not castes, for there was considerable mobility among them.

Each class had norms of behavior ascribed to it; thus class related to status. The lowest classes were those thought overly concerned with self-interest, the merchants; but their wealth eventually brought them status. Traditionally the highest status was accorded those of high learning and good moral character. The distinction between the ruler and the ruled, as well as the distinction between mental and manual labor, was consistently upheld throughout the history of Chinese social thought.

CONFUCIAN SOCIAL STRATA

Although the process by which a person attained office has its own history—which must be studied separately to understand the development of the class of officials—it is widely accepted that officialdom, as a class, has comprised the ruling administrators of ancient China.[41]

Ping-ti points out that despite the fluid nature of class membership, skill and wealth remain extremely important.[42] But Ho does not address whether his four functional divisions in society have common political interests that they attempt to articulate in the political arena; his analyses are couched in Weberian, not Marxian concepts. Men may lose their position as members of a ruling class because of a change in personal fortune, withdrawal from the world while in mourning, or because poor advice was given to a senior official, but the character and structure of the gentry, as a class of administrators, remained consistent.[43] Arthur F. Wright and Dennis Twitchett, however, tell us that Confucian scholars were "a very small elite dispersed over a vast land but bound together by common interests, kinship ties, and political connections."[44]

T'ung-tsu Ch'u, in contrast to Ho, sees five manifestations of social class in China:

> (1) The members of society were judged and ranked in a hierarchical order on the basis of commonly accepted values. . . . (2) There were indications of class consciousness: persons of similar status thought of each other as equals belonging to the same group (with interests opposed to another group). (3) Members of the same class had a similar style of life that was distinct from others. They were aware of such symbols of prestige (dress, modes of travel) and made an effort to cultivate and maintain them. (4) Members of the same class were considered equals or near-equals, and therefore were acceptable to each other for social interaction. A person married within his (or her) class. (5) Status groups enjoyed certain privileges. Sumptuary laws were formulated to guarantee these groups the monopoly of such things as style of houses, clothing, carriages, and so forth.[45]

Ch'u, however, believed that the basic unit of social class in China was the family, not the individual.[46] The social class system extended through the entire kinship net of the extended family.[47]

Access to the gentry class remained relatively stable; and although it changed from a system that was based solely on merit and learning to a system in which privilege could be bought, membership in the ruling class was never totally fixed. Fixed-class statuses applied only to the children of certain families—prostitutes, entertainers, police, and the servants of magistrates—who could not take part in the imperial examination system.[48] The castelike aristocracy, at the same time, began to break down. Munro traces this development to the emergence of the Confucian system and the development of a wealthy merchant class between the fourth and sixth century B.C.[49] Brian McKnight agrees that the development of a merchant class broke the castelike nature of China's aristocracy; but he sees this as a later development that took place in the Sung dynasty.[50]

These points are reinforced by Karl Wittfogel's analysis of the land distribution system in China. Wittfogel, in *Oriental Despotism*, notes that because inherited land was divided equally among all sons, the wealth of a family could change between generations.[51] The insistence upon equal distribution of inheritance of land tended to shrink landholdings across time, leading to considerable fluidity in the composition of gentry classes. Fei Xiaotong also stresses that the system of inheritance tends to lend fluidity to the composition of the gentry but notes that the political power of the gentry was generally associated with their relationship to a member of the bureaucracy (in their family) rather than with their wealth.[52] It should be noted that according to Fei, political power was related more to the position one held in the bureaucracy or to one's family influence over the bureaucracy than to wealth or the ownership of land. However, where there is extreme wealth in a family across generations, these observations about the lack of correlation between landownership and gentry class membership across generations may not apply.

PROSCRIBED BEHAVIOR

Underlying this continuity in class relations, a continuity that T'ung-tsu Ch'u tells us extended to the very dress and manners of each class, was a system of ritualized behavior expected of all members of society.[53] The Confucian system specified how sets of relations were to be conducted: relations between ruler and ruled (emperor and subject), father and son, husband and wife, elder and younger brother (or sister), and friends were to be handled in a set manner, with special terms of address for each person that denoted rank or position in the social hierarchy. These relations extended to teacher-pupil, apprentice-craftsman, and so forth. Almost any relationship of authority based on age or expertise was bound by the system. This system for ritual behavior between persons, known as *xiao* (or filial piety), and the insistence upon correct name and action, can be traced to earlier than three thousand years before the establishment of the People's Republic of China.[54]

In addition to the observance of filial piety, there are four other cardinal virtues that a Chinese adult was to observe in traditional society. *Ren*, formed of the ideographs that represent man and the number two, is generally interpreted to mean that between two people there should be a correct relationship: interpersonal relations should be based on a combination of filial piety and fraternal love, duty, and a desire to observe the social amenities. But to observe these procedures, to ensure that *ren* was part of a relationship, a person must submit to *li*, or prescribed etiquette involving a show of respect, deference, and reverence. The observation of *li* was particularly important with respect to an individual's parents, and injunctions for good behavior extended for years after the death of a parent. A person of good manners, one deserving to rule, must also exhibit a sense of righteousness, or *yi*. The meaning of *yi* is that one must do as one ought morally, out of a genuine desire to be a moral person, rather than to do what one would like to do for personal gain or profit. The same *yi* is used in the character for an uprising or revolt, *qiyi*, which provides a moral justification for revolt against unjust rule. Finally, *xin*, which means good faith or sincerity in deeds, is required of a person fit to rule.

These five cardinal virtues of behavior were part of the daily education of a Chinese youth. Indeed, the ideograph meaning filial piety forms part of the ideograph that means instruction or teaching, *jiao*. Not only was education based on these principles, but the content of examinations for office was based upon the ability to recall and comment on essays about the five cardinal virtues.

Perhaps the most apropos statement relationship between the older Confucian virtues and their influence in contemporary China was made by Donald J. Munro:

> Under the Confucian influence in the past, a person might be thought of as belonging to the group ''younger brothers,'' which is defined in terms of the group ''elder brothers,'' and part of the definition of each consists of the duties it owes or the expectations to which it is entitled from the other. Today, we would call these social roles. In contemporary China, individuals are identified in terms of classes or subclasses, such as lower-middle peasant, which is defined in terms of other groups (e.g., landlord or rich peasant). Each per-

> son belongs to a series of ever more comprehensive groups. The Confucian younger brother might belong also to the group of "superior men" that is defined in terms of the morally backward "common people" and also to the group of culturally advanced Han people that is defined by reference to culturally retarded barbarians.[55]

Munro shows how the Confucian tradition, a legacy that survives in the family and the village, extends into contemporary society. Roles are fixed, but social nature is influenced by class position in the Marxist interpretation. Learning still occurs through the imitation of models, but the models have changed and, in contemporary China, have a class nature.[56]

The imperial examination system, with its ritualized essays, its insistence on duplicative thought, and its requirement for rote memorization, is another example of an institution that survives, in modified form, in contemporary China. The imperial examination can be traced to a rudimentary examination system instituted in 400 B.C.[57] Today one must look to Party schools, with their requirements to memorize large sections of text and interpret them properly, as the legacy of the examination system. Given the stability of these institutions and their inculcation into the norms of the family and state, one can well imagine that their influence is not easily erased. Perhaps these institutions should not be so easily erased, for they are what gives Chinese society its character. As Joseph R. Levenson suggests, all class labels, all criteria for cadre behavior, and even literary form in contemporary China must be interpreted in light of this foundation.[58]

Although Marxist labels are new, the labeling of persons or families for generations at a time is a long-established tradition in China. When Communist Party organs order study groups to review official documents in order to ensure that all Party members are able to reflect the official position and intepretation, that is a continuation of long-standing practice. When the Party Central Committee insists upon democratic centralism, the action parallels the older practice of requiring ministers and local officials unequivocally to support decisions of the central government. When the cries go out to rectify the workstyle of communist cadre, it is parallel to the older call to rectify names and to ensure that people act in accordance with what is expected of their position. Being and name must correspond. With this as a basis, the next chapter presents an interpretation of Maoist epistemology. The Party analysis of class in contemporary China is grounded on the traditional concept of order in society. The traits of the individual and the traits of classes, even the way that these traits are transmitted, rely upon a Marxism that retains part of this earlier conception of order.

3

Epistemology and Class: The Party Line

The official view of class in China today is founded on a perspective adopted from the lectures and writings of Mao Zedong. The works of Marx, Engels, Lenin, and Stalin, of course, contributed to the official view. There is no single text to which one can point that exhaustively analyzes the question of social class, the nature and methods of human knowledge of social stratification, or the way in which the Chinese Communist Party engages in class analysis. Instead, one must turn to a series of works by Mao dating from 1926, but the most important of which were composed during the period of the War of Resistance against Japan (1937–1945) at the Communist guerrilla base in Yanan.[1] These texts were used for military and political education and without doubt formed the content of cadre political study at the Anti-Japanese Military and Political College in Yanan. They remain, with the commentaries on them, the major texts for political study and education in China today.

The CCP Eleventh Central Committee's Sixth Plenum, in its landmark summation of Party history, cites more than forty separate texts that form the core of Mao Zedong thought.[2] Before one can understand the official line on class by the Party, it is first necessary to understand the Russian and German classical Marxist works and, second, to understand the epistemology in Mao's texts. Together they form the underpinnings of theory for the Party and for the educational system in China today.[3] Political understanding and the symbolic universe of political dialogue in China are a result of years of continuous political study sessions and education based on materials that inculcate

Mao's epistemology.[4] Before examining Mao's work we will briefly review what Marx, Engels, Lenin, and Stalin said about class.

MARX AND ENGELS ON CLASS

Marx's "The Eighteenth Brumaire of Louis Bonaparte" provides some of the most lucid definitional criteria for social class available in Marx's works.[5] First and foremost, according to this work members of the same class occupy common positions in the economic mode of production.[6] That is, they are all related in their work to certain means of production in the same way, through similar relations of ownership. Each class leads a separate way of life and a separate cultural existence, with social relationships that extend across local or regional lines. Moreover, for a group to form a class, its members must be conscious, on a societywide basis, of themselves as a class. In other words, they must make the transition from the "in-itself" to the "for-itself," becoming a "class-for-itself."[7]

Within society these classes always occupy a conflicting position and have hostile interests with respect to other classes. Finally, there must be some form of political organization before a class is constituted, not only to allow a social formation fully to achieve consciousness as a class but to articulate its interests as these interests are opposed to other classes.

Marx views classes as being formed by social relations of production that are historically related to the different means of production in a given epoch or period. These means of production are influenced by the technology available within this epoch and constitute a mode of production: tribal, slave, feudal, capitalist, socialist, or communist. The central assertion in Marx's thesis is that social relations of production are responses by humankind to the environment.[8] The responses to the environment are grounded in nature and therefore constitute an economic basis for society. As a part of these responses, social relations of production develop within a framework of legitimated authority, allowing one class to exercise hegemony over another or others. *This power is based on the ownership of the means of production.*

According to Marx, the capitalist mode of production comprises three major classes: "the owners of mere labor power, the owners of capital, and landlords."[9] At the same time, he recognizes constituent strata within each major class division (e.g., a dairy owner, who is a capitalist and also a landlord). In the first chapter of *The German Ideology* Marx and Engels make the point that it is the ability of one class to appropriate the labor of another that is the basis of class struggle in history, and of the antagonisms that exist among classes.[10]

LENIN

Lenin expanded Marx's views by positing specific relationships between the development of a class-conscious group of workers (the proletariat as a "class-for-itself") and its leadership: a centralized party, which he calls the vanguard, that acts as the "avante-garde of the proletariat."[11] In addition, Lenin developed a refined theory of the relationship of classes (particularly the ruling class) to the state, providing the political theory of class lacking in Marx.[12] We owe to Lenin the fullest operating definition of classes accepted in Marxist literature—the definition on which the CCP bases its views:

> Classes are large groups of people which differ from each other by the place they occupy in a historically determined system of production, by their relation (in most cases fixed and formulated by law) to the means of production, by their role in the social organization of labor, and, consequently, by the dimensions and method of acquiring the share of social wealth of which they dispose. Classes are groups of people, one of which can appropriate the labor of another, owing to the different places they occupy in a definite system of social economy.[13]

Whereas Marx had little to say about the administration of society after a socialist revolution, Lenin specified ways that the bourgeoisie, specialists and state officials, landowners, and the intelligentsia could be controlled and used by the state under the direction of the vanguard party. The state, according to Lenin, is an organ for class rule; a vehicle for the oppression of one class by another.[14] This is true even after the revolution, when the state is used to legitimate forces of repression to prevent a resurgence of the former ruling classes.[15] Lenin conceptualized the state as created by society in order to manage or reconcile its own inherent antagonisms and contradictions. However, because the conflicting interests of classes are irreconcilable, the state "has a tendency to increasingly alienate itself from society and stand above it as a separate power.''[16] It was Stalin, however, who wrestled with the theoretical question of how to reconcile the continued existence of classes under socialism.

STALIN

Faced with the continued existence of social classes in a society with a goal of communism twenty years after a revolution, Stalin had to develop a theoretical justification for this phenomenon. To this day the existence of classes in a socialist society, including the one in China, is justified on the basis of a formula developed by Stalin in 1936. In that year, in a speech on the new Soviet constitution to the Congress of Soviets, Stalin declared that there were no longer any antagonistic classes in socialist society.[17] Instead, according to Stalin, two new working classes had emerged in the Soviet Union. These classes corresponded to the two forms of ownership in that country: collective ownership and state ownership (or ownership by the whole people).[18] Stalin asserted that class would not be eliminated under socialism but that the exploitive relationship between owners and non-owners of the means of production had been destroyed by the nature of socialist society. Because exploitive relationships had been eliminated, he theorized that classes would continue to exist under socialism, but these classes no longer had antagonistic interests.

Despite the purges and murders of Stalin's regime, and Stalin's subsequent denunciation by the Communist Party of the Soviet Union (the CCP issued no similar denunciation), his speech stands as a formal acknowledgment that there are classes under socialism, an acknowledgment that has not been renounced to this date. As we shall see, it is an admission that was accepted by Mao Zedong and still has currency in the CCP.

THE CHINESE COMMUNIST VIEW

Many of the attitudes toward class reflected in CCP texts of the Yanan period were already present in Mao's earlier works and are contained in postrevolution works. The key point for this book is that the isolation of the Party at Yanan, the development of what the party calls the ''Yanan Spirit'' (*Yanan jingshen*), and the protracted use of these texts as the basis for class analysis have transformed them into canons, the knowledge of which has become a key criterion for Party membership.[19]

Because of the nature of CCP political study sessions, in which people are required to quote these key texts from memory and repeat the official interpretation of the Party, these texts form the official epistemology of the CCP and the nation. The texts are *catechized*: all problems and questions are analyzed according to the method in the texts; political discourse is conducted in the language of these texts. Consequently, the language of the texts forms the means for political communication in China; the epistemology implicit in the texts dictates how class differences are understood.

Mao's Ideas on Class

The attitude of Mao and the attitude of the Party toward class has changed periodically, making it more difficult to discuss the intent of official analyses. Richard Kraus has summarized the changes in this way: "The Chinese Communist Party . . . subtly transformed class into stratification. Although class designations were intended to make concrete the abstractions of Marxist theory . . . they unavoidably assumed the character of a hierarchy of social stratification."[20] Kraus goes on to say that the Party has stratified society in several ways: by occupational rank, by property ownership, according to political consciousness, even according to family designation or label.[21] John Starr also finds the derivation of a general definition of class from the works of Mao or from Party documents equally problematic:

> Mao came to regard politics and ideology as having an effect equally important as that of economics in altering the nature and composition of classes in a socialist society. This is particularly evident in his discussion of a change in class status stemming from the remolding of an individual's economic, political, and ideological orientations through revolutionary education and "socialist transformation." The same idea of multi-causality is also evident in his treatment of the reverse of this process—the change of class status that he sees as stemming from the deterioration of an individual's economic, political, and ideological orientations.[22]

Kraus and Starr, however, have missed an important point: although the object or focus of class *struggle* has changed, the method of separating classes has remained consistent since 1926.[23] This method is at the heart of the solution to understanding the shifting meaning of the concept "class." The Party line has varied, depending upon whether orthodox or more pragmatic Party members given to a revision of the tests were in power; but the dialectical method used in class analysis has been a constant. We will explore the essence of this method so that the reader may understand the official definition of class offered by the CCP today.

From the time Mao Zedong began systematically to analyze classes in China, there was never a concise, definitive statement about what criteria with respect to the ownership of the means of production were to be primary in the analysis. Factors other than the ownership of the means of production were often considered by Mao to be more important—both for the analysis of classes and for the formation of alliances that fostered the Communist cause—primarily attitudes toward the Communist Revolution.

Mao did not start his formal analysis of class by demonstrating the relationships between property ownership and political interest in Chinese society, a relationship that is the basic question to be asked in a Marxist analysis. Instead Mao asked, "Who are our enemies? Who are our friends?"[24] Having posed these questions Mao proceeded, on the one hand, to dichotomize the population of China according to what he perceived their stance to be with regard to the Party (with a concern for potential alliances) while, on the other hand, he delineated classes and strata. The salient criterion Mao used was the analysis of friends and enemies:

> This is a question of the first importance for the revolution. The basic reason why all previous revolutionary struggles achieved so little was their failure to unite with real friends in order to attack real enemies. A revolutionary party is the guide for the masses and no revolution ever succeeds when the revolutionary party leads them astray. To ensure that we will definitely achieve success in our revolution and will not lead the masses astray, we must pay attention to uniting with our real friends in order to attack our real enemies. To distinguish real friends from real enemies we must make a general analysis of the economic status of the various classes in Chinese society and of their respective attitudes toward the revolution.[25]

Mao listed six classes in his 1926 "Analysis of Classes in Chinese Society."[26] However, Mao recognized that these classes are composed of various strata; and between the analysis of classes and other politico-economic investigations, he derived twenty-four strata. These strata were further subdivided into eighteen substrata, but the list is still not inclusive; the positions of some sectors of society are only implied (see table 1).[27]

Mao avoided specific mention of the traditional declassed elements of Chinese society such as prostitutes, singers, actors, geomancers and fortune-tellers. Perhaps he associated these with either the "superstitious" and "feudal" legacy of ancient China or with the presence of foreign imperial influences in China; but certainly he ignored them in his analysis.[28] Mao did devote some discussion to the criminal elements from secret societies, whom he believed could be revolutionized because they had turned to secret organizations to flee exploitation.[29] Persons from these backgrounds figured in the process of assigning class labels and the analysis of class background in Shanxi Province during the spring and summer of 1948. According to Hinton, after the revolution peasants were sympathetic to persons from declassed backgrounds.[30]

Class analysis and class consciousness came to be determined "less by the stage of development of production by social individuals, than by the political motivation of members of a socialist state."[31] The "big landlord" and "big comprador" bourgeoisie were on the opposite side of the class struggle from the Party because Mao believed they were "tied to the international bourgeoisie," and "their existence was utterly incompatible with the aims of the Chinese revolution."[32] Mao also condemned the official government bureaucracy that supported municipal control and authority, as well as the banking and financial infrastructure, because he viewed these elements as dependent on the landlords and compradors. These strata were not enemies because of their ownership of the means of production; rather, they were viewed as enemies because they had an identity of interests with the ruling class.[33]

Although they too owned the means of production, the "middle bourgeoisie," Chinese capitalists in the town and the countryside, were not necessarily placed into the category of "enemies."[34] Mao dichotomized both urban and rural capitalists—and those employed by capitalists whose employment served their interests—into those who might in the future support the revolution and those who would not. The operant criterion seemed to be whether the individual lived from an

Table 1
Mao Zedong's Class Designations

1. Landlord Class and Comprador Class
   Strata: Big landlords
   Smaller landlords
   Bankrupt landlords who do not work
   Comprador–Chinese manager of a foreign commercial establishment
   –Senior employee of a foreign commercial establishment
   Representatives of the landlord class such as warlords, major local tyrants, senior officials, rent collectors more economically well off than a middle peasant, evil gentry [an undefined term].

2. Middle Bourgeoisie
   Strata: Urban capitalists
   Rural capitalists
   Enlightened gentry [supportive of communist revolution]
   Nonenlightened gentry [foes of communist revolution]
   [Implied strata: higher government functionaries, lawyers, university teachers, higher intellectuals, office managers]

3. Petty Bourgeoisie
   Strata: Owner-peasants
   Master handicraftsmen
   Lower intellectuals such as students, primary and secondary school teachers, small lawyers, small traders (in family business), lower government functionaries, office clerks.

4. Semiproletariat
   Strata: Upper semiowner peasants
   Middle semiowner peasants
   Lower semiowner peasants
   Poor peasants
   Small handicraftsmen
   Shop assistants
   Peddlers

5. Proletariat
   Strata: Industrial workers (railway, mining, maritime, transport, textile)
   Dockworkers
   Rickshawmen
   Rural day, month, or annual workers

6. Lumpenproletariat
   Strata: Peasants with no land
   Craftsmen with no work
   Industrial workers with no work

income that was solely dependent on the employment of others, including the employment of agricultural labor. In fact, based on the account of the process of assigning class labels in *Fanshen*, one can almost substitute the term "exploitation" for "employment" in any of Mao's texts.[35] Interestingly, although Mao categorizes such persons—primary and secondary school teachers, "small lawyers," "small traders," office clerks, and lower government functionaries—as petty-bourgeoisie, such categories are imprecise and only invite more questions.[36]

How does one differentiate a "small lawyer" from a "big lawyer"? What is the difference between a "small trader" and the owner of a small business? Explicit Party instructions or explanations for such distinctions are absent. In October 1933, in the document "How to Differentiate the Classes in the Rural Areas," Mao provides only the most generic criteria.[37] However, the definitions in that document are all relative and contain such statements as this one, which is the criterion for identifying a rich peasant:

> The rich peasant generally has rather more and better instruments of production and more liquid capital than the average and engages in labor himself, but always relies on exploitation for part or even the major part of his income. . . . A person who owns a fair amount of good land, farms some of it himself without hiring labor, but exploits other peasants by means of land rent, loan interest or in other ways, shall also be treated as a rich peasant.[38]

Within Party directives there probably are detailed formulae for making such determinations: one Chinese informant stated that the criterion established by the Party for labeling a person a capitalist was the possession of bank assets of over 5000 *yuan*.[39] Hinton provided a formula that was used in Long Bow Village to separate strata of the peasantry from rich peasants and landlords.[40] Certainly the employment of workers outside the immediate family was a factor in determining a class label; but the overriding criterion employed by Mao was whether the individual was likely to oppose the revolution or not.

The question of how to analyze classes in urban areas received more murky treatment. The semiproletariat consisted of five strata: (1) the semiowner peasant (further divided into three substrata); (2) poor peasants (who own no implements and little or no land and must sell labor); (3) small handicraftsmen; (4) shop assistants; and (5) peddlers.[41]

Mao believed that even though some members of the semiproletariat owned the means of production, they were a class that was extremely receptive to Party propaganda because of their impoverishment.

Despite his later concentration on the potential for revolution in the countryside, Mao was still a doctrinaire Marxist-Leninist: he initially identified completely with the industrial proletarian class, which he characterized as "the force in our revolution"—although in 1927, at the time of his study, they numbered only about two million.[42] This reliance on the proletariat is an example of his early orthodoxy. There was confusion, however, about who constituted the proletariat. The rural proletariat, according to Mao, included day, month, and annual farm laborers. Yet he admitted that they might at times own land or farming implements, which, of course, are means of production.[43]

This imprecision about the composition of classes is only compounded by translations of articles by Stuart Schram. In a section extracted from a 1926 article that apparently forms the basis for the official version of "Analysis of Classes in Chinese Society," Mao listed eight separate classes of people in the Chinese countryside alone.[44] This original article did not even consider what other classes Mao might have identified in the city. One can only conclude that at that stage of his life Mao was clear neither about what constituted a class in the Marxian sense nor about how to differentiate the classes in China. He was, however, very clear about identifying whether groups were friends or enemies of the "people":

> To sum up, it can be seen that our enemies are all those in league with imperialism—the landlords, the bureaucrats, the comprador class, the big landlord class, and the reactionary section of the intelligentsia attached to them. The leading force in our revolution is the industrial proletariat. Our closest friends are the entire semi-proletariat and petty-bourgeoisie. As for the vacillating middle bourgeoisie, their right-wing may become our enemy and their left-wing may become our friends—but we must be constantly on our guard and not let them create confusion in our ranks.[45]

Even these statements are not definitive; by 1948, when Mao required the support of the landlords and intellectuals in the last push for a total Communist victory in China, he established new criteria for class relations. In an inner-Party directive he decided to make an effort to win over the national bourgeoisie, suggesting publicly that the

Communist Party was by no means anticapitalist. "Its aim," said Mao, "was not to abolish capitalism in general."[46] Mao suggested a temporary united front policy to win the cooperation of landlords and bourgeoisie, redesignating them "enlightened gentry with democratic leanings," and redoubled Party efforts to win over intellectuals.[47]

Faced with these inconsistencies, one must either conclude that Mao would resort to any means of duplicity to advance the revolution, including blatant lies, or that Mao and the inner leadership of the party had based their policy decisions on some means of viewing the world other than a system based on the analysis of ownership of the means of production. The following interpretation of a series of documents and addresses by Mao provides an explanation of the epistemology used in class analysis.

The Maoist Theory of Knowledge

Mao's analysis of classes and of society is built on two pillars: a theory of practice and a theory of contradiction. Both of these theories were first expounded at the Anti-Japanese Military and Political College in Yanan and later published in essay form.[48] As Schurmann has pointed out, "the fact that these two essays are usually referred to together not only indicates the centrality of the notion of contradictions in Chinese communist ideology, but also that contradictions are regarded as having practical functions."[49] Even before recognition was restored to Mao's works by the Communist Party in December 1983, the essays "On Practice" and "On Contradiction" were acknowledged as the basis for all understanding in contemporary Chinese philosophy.[50] The Marxist theorist Wu Jiang, in fact, states that "the essence of Mao's theory of epistemology is contained in 'On Practice.' "[51] In a major commentary published for the anniversary of the Party, "On Contradiction" was again acknowledged as fundamental to Chinese Marxist theory.[52]

Mao believed that only through human activity in material production could mankind understand "phenomena, the properties and the laws of nature, and the relationships between himself and nature" as well as "relations that exist between man and man."[53] He characterized this understanding as the perceptual stage of knowledge (*renshi ganxing de jieduan*), where the senses gain impressions of the outside world. Here Mao emphasizes that perception is always of something.

Knowledge cannot proceed from the mind alone but must involve the cognition of something external; perception is interactive.

Mao was also convinced that only by verifying ideas developed from repeated human activity (or practice, *shijian*) could humankind ensure the correct understanding of the "laws of the external world."[54] The human mind begins to develop a grasp of the relationships between sense perceptions through further practice until the ability to make judgments and reach conclusions is developed. This, then, becomes the rational stage of cognition (*lixing renshi de jieduan*), which reveals the nature of the surrounding world and its "inner contradictions." Understanding the material world involves a process of continual advance and progress that, according to Mao, develops because of (1) the internal contradictions (*neibu maodun*) inherent in the nature of the world and (2) the struggle between these inherent contradictions.[55] Each stage of interaction with the phenomenal world leads to a deepening knowledge of it until, through a "leap" (*ji fei yue*), a general theory is developed, tested through practice, and refined. Mao summarized the process this way:

> Discover the truth through practice, and again through practice verify and develop the truth. Start from perceptual knowledge and actively develop it into rational knowledge; then start from rational knowledge and actively guide revolutionary practice to change both the subjective and the objective world. Practice, knowledge, again practice, and again knowledge. This form repeats itself in endless cycles, and with each cycle the content or practice and knowledge rises to a higher level. Such is the whole of dialectical-materialistic theory of knowledge, and such is the dialectical-materialist theory of the unity of knowing and doing.[56]

Ideas that are not grounded in experience are meaningless; theories that are not tested in practice are likely to be incorrect. Social theory in modern China can be tested only in revolutionary practice: this is the content of Mao's essay. It seems to offer the opportunity to continually revise theory in the light of new conditions or unsuccessful revolutionary practice—a built-in revisionism based upon what, in empirical thought, is recognized as the scientific method. This practice is supposed to reveal the inner contradictions in the world, which become clear because "every process, whether in the realm of nature or society, progresses and develops by reason of its internal contradiction and struggle, and the movement of human knowledge should also develop and progress along with it.''[57] Based on this dialectical process Mao hypothesized that the contradictory nature of the external world must be understood before ''rational knowledge'' can be achieved, hence the companion essay ''On Contradiction.''

In documenting his thoughts on contradictions, Mao, citing Engels and Lenin, professed a belief that ''all things, all aspects of life,'' have opposite tendencies that are both mutually exclusive and interdependent.[58] The result of this opposition is a struggle between contradictions that pushes forward the development of things and the world. In the essay Mao offers an example of the interdependence of opposites by analyzing the broad concept of ''war,'' which is formed of the opposites of ''offence and defence, advance and retreat, victory and defeat,'' each of which depends upon the other to provide its definition.[59] The unity of opposites, however, is not a new concept to China. As Starr remarks, both the *Yi-Jing* (*Book of Changes*) and the *Dao De Jing* are based on the mutually interdependent nature of opposites.[60]

Consider this passage translated from the *Dao De Jing*:

> All in the world know the beauty of the beautiful, and in doing this they have (the idea of) what ugliness is; they all know the skill of the skillful, and in doing this they have (the idea of) what the want of skill is. So it is that existence and non-existence give birth the one to (the idea of) the other; that difficulty and ease produce the one (the idea of) the other; that length and shortness fashion out of the one the figure of the other; that the musical notes and tones become harmonious through the relation of one with another; and that being before and being behind give the idea of following one another.[61]

The *Yi-Jing* is equally specific about the role of change and opposites in defining concepts in the universe. The book emphasizes the complementary nature of opposites in the universe, demonstrating how opposites give way, through conflict, to ceaseless change.[62] Thus when Mao uses the dialectic as the source of knowledge, he seizes a mode of understanding that is compatible with the traditional philosophical systems of China: these emphasize cyclical change as the only permanent force in history.

As Levenson pointed out, the exclusive categories of Marxist struggle are not the same as the traditional forms of harmony between opposites in Confucian thought.[63] However, the differences in content are insignificant when compared to the vast similarities in form between the two modes of thought.

Mao's theory of contradictions depends on the ability of the user both to understand that every concept—everything, universally—has contradictions and to discern, through study and analysis, the particular contradictions in any situation. Now reified, the theory has been turned into the officially acceptable method for social and political analysis in China. Every problem, whether social, legal, or economic, is approached employing the dialectical formula of "one dividing into two (*yi fen wei er*)."[64] The essence of this process involves taking a thing and conceptually dividing it into two parts that have contradictory elements. The interlocutor then proceeds to respond to a series of questions with respect to the phenomenon: What is the contradiction? What is the antagonistic nature of the contradiction? How can the contradiction be unified (rendered nonantagonistic)?[65]

Here the introduction of the question of antagonism is critical. Mao stated that contradictions may develop from a nonantagonistic nature into an antagonistic one, depending on the conditions that exist in the world.[66] He notes that within the Party are persons who think correctly and persons who think incorrectly, but because all of these persons are Party members, the contradictions are initially nonantagonistic. If those whose thought is judged to be incorrect do not modify their positions, they may become guilty of harboring thoughts that are antagonistic to what the Party identifies as the interests of the proletariat. With respect to the economic conditions of China in 1937, Mao put it this way:

> Economically, the contradiction between town and country is an extremely antagonistic one both in capitalist society, where under the rule of the bourgeoisie the towns ruthlessly plunder the countryside, and in the Kuomintang (Guomindang) areas in China, where under the rule of foreign imperialism and the Chinese big comprador bourgeoisie the towns most rapaciously plunder the countryside. But in a socialist country and in our revolutionary base areas, this antagonistic contradiction has changed into one that is non-antagonistic; and when communist society is reached it will be abolished.[67]

The alert student of "Mao Zedong thought" will recognize in this passage the threads of ideas that later were woven into two other essays: in "On the Ten Major Relationships," one can see the core-periphery relationship of the city and countryside; "On the Correct Handling of Contradictions among the People" shows how a contradiction becomes nonantagonistic.[68] Schurmann discusses three separate applications of the theory of contradictions by the CCP that are extensions of this essay: (1) it is the basis for social analysis according to the dialectical method; (2) it is used to polarize small groups in discussion sessions and to throw them together in struggle (the basis of thought reform); and (3) it is the basis of Party insistence on the contradictory concepts of democratic centralism and democratic dictatorship.[69]

In the essay "On the Correct Handling of Contradictions among the People," Mao resorts to the same formula he used in his 1926 class analysis of Chinese society. First, one must differentiate between "ourselves" (friends) and "the enemy" by asking the question "Who are our friends?"[70] One can then begin to deal with the classes in China according to the category in which they fall. Contradictions among the "people," who in 1957 were defined as "the classes, strata and social groups which favor, support and work for the cause of socialist construction," are nonantagonistic and may be resolved through discussion, education, and political work.[71] Contradictions between the Party, as the vanguard of the proletariat, and the enemies of the people ("the social forces and groups which resist the socialist revolution and are hostile to or sabotage socialist construction") were, according to Mao, always antagonistic.[72]

This method of analyzing classes does not consider the relationship of a social group to the means of production as having primary importance. It is a relative definition based on the bifurcation of classes according to their likely stance with respect to specific Party policies in any given historical period. During the war against Japan anyone who sided against the Japanese was one of the "people," regardless of his or her relationship to the means of production. During the period of land reform, the enemy became those who sided against the Party policy on land redistribution. During the antirightist campaign, the enemy became those who criticized the Party for its dogmatic control of aesthetics and culture. During collectivization, the enemy became those who opposed the creation of communes. A 1952 article from a Chinese journal states explicitly that the real method of analyzing classes was to "judge the attitude of a class toward the Chinese revolution."[73] Economic position (wealth) and the position of an individual in relations of production were only secondary considerations. In a second article in the same journal also concerned with providing guidance for the conduct of class analysis during the land reform program in China, the author relies upon Mao's basic questions, "Who are our friends? Who are our enemies?"[74]

During the period of land reform, all Chinese were classified, or "capped," according to their class status. Kraus has referred to this process as the creation of a caste system based upon determination of family background.[75] The entire system grew so ponderous that more than sixty designations of class were used during the period of "capping."[76] Adults were classified according to their "personal status" (*ge ren chengfen*) determined by their behavior, social relations of production, and political attitudes toward the revolution and toward land reform. Children and adolescents below the age of eighteen, or those still attending school, received a classification based on the personal status of one of the members of their family, which created a category known as "family status" (*jiating chengfen*). This complicated process depended on the Party committee empowered to recommend status as much as it depended on popular agreement, but the fundamental question asked was whether the subjects were "friends" or "enemies" of the Party and the revolution.[77]

The Method of Class Analysis

Those who have followed the past three decades of political history in the People's Republic of China have been subjected to an overpowering demonstration of the Orwellian ability of the single ruling party to assign labels to members of classes. Heroes of the formative period of the Communist Party have been labeled class enemies. Leaders of the Communist Revolution have been labeled class enemies. The marshals who led the Party in the war against Japan have been labeled class enemies. The president of the People's Republic of China has been labeled a class enemy. Deng Xiaoping, the current ideological leader of the country, has been repeatedly purged and reinstated. Over one-quarter of the people authorized by the Party to be attacked by mass organizations during the Great Proletarian Cultural Revolution have been rehabilitated. Yet in all cases the same authority has been invoked in the conduct of class analysis: dialectical and historical materialism and Mao's theory of contradictions.

In the Party's view, society is first and foremost a response to the environment—the material world. But, following Mao's formula, the Party still insists that society be divided into "the people" and "enemies." At the same time, because social development is viewed as a historical process by communists, society may also be divided another way, into two other components: a socialist component and a capitalist component. According to the Party's official line, because the historical stage of communism has not been reached, one cannot yet speak of a communist component of society, only of communist ideas. Between the capitalist and communist components of Chinese society there are antagonistic relations. Thus those in socialist society may be classed either with "the people" or with "the enemy."

How, then, the reader may ask, does the Party account for the united front with the national bourgeoisie? Was that simply an expedient, the big lie, to gain the temporary cooperation of the bourgeoisie against the Guomindang? It may have been that, but it was theoretically justifiable in Mao's eyes because one must leave the realm of social relations and move to the realm of ideas to understand class analysis. A judicious reading of the major documents used for study by the Party reveals a division of both capitalist society and socialist society into groups with mutually opposing sets of ideas—socialist ideas and capitalist ideas. Some persons in socialist society still maintain capitalist (rightist) ideas; others maintain socialist ideas. In capitalist society the same process of "one thing dividing into two" takes place; therefore capitalist society is also composed of people with capitalist ideas and socialist ideas.

What of social relations in capitalist society? Capitalist ideas and socialist ideas are, of course, antagonistic. This is why Marxists insist that capitalism will collapse of its own accord; they theorize that capitalist society will necessarily produce people with socialist ideas. At the theoretical level, Mao can suggest that the national bourgeoisie are part of "the people" because those people in capitalist society who can be reeducated to have socialist ideas will have a relationship that, although contradictory, is nonantagonistic with those in socialist society who have socialist ideas. When the Party decided to attack the president of the republic, Liu Shaoqi, the decision had to be justified theoretically. Liu's ideological differences with Mao were theoretically justifiable because there are antagonistic relations between those in a socialist society with capitalist ideas and those in a socialist society with socialist ideas. Persons with capitalist ideas in a socialist society could be attacked because their ideas were compatible with capitalist societies. Liu therefore becomes an enemy of the people. Ideological arguments may remain arguments among the people, but the argument with Liu was more fundamental.

An entire segment of the Party was reclassified from the category of "the people" to the category of "the enemy." Along with the reclassification as class enemies, they were identified as targets for class struggle. While at the time there was an inner-party struggle going on over the distribution of power, the reclassification was more than just a power play—it was an action that was theoretically correct, justified by the Party's, and Mao's, epistemology.

This process of redesignating forms of behavior and sets of ideas as noncommunist, and therefore necessarily capitalist, is best illustrated through the class analysis performed by the Party after Mao's death. At this time, driven by the need to quell popular dissent over the distribution of wealth and privilege among Party members, the Party began a purge. Behavior that would be considered criminal in Western eyes was labeled a reflection of capitalist influences in socialist society but was not considered a reflection of class stratification in socialist China. This process provides the basis for the analysis of class by the Party and is grounded on the epistemology in Mao's theory of contradictions as well as the historico-genesis of the Yanan period.

THE CONTEMPORARY LINE ON CLASS

Since the Third Plenary Session of the CCP's Eleventh Central Committee, held in December 1978, there has been a revision of the Party's Cultural Revolution insistence on the need for a focus on struggle as a key aspect in the analysis of classes in China. This revision, based on the application of Mao's theory of contradictions, is predicated in theory on the coexistence of both capitalist ideas and socialist ideas in a state of continual tension in socialist society. Most recently, dishonest acts by Party members and private citizens have been attributed to the intrusion of capitalist ideas from abroad. In general, the CCP has failed to make a viable analysis of class in socialist China.

The reading notes to Volume V of Mao's *Selected Works*, prepared by Hua Guofeng, presaged the general reassessment of the role of classes and class struggle in socialist society by the CCP Central Committee. In 1977, while he occupied positions as chairman of the CCP and premier of the People's Republic, Hua accused the Gang of Four of failing to discern clearly the differences between two types of contradiction—"those among the people and those between ourselves and the enemy."[78] Hua used this formula to explain that classes are represented by the Party, and that class struggle in socialist society is reflected in class struggle in the Communist Party. He simply reversed the accusations that had been directed against the "capitalist roaders" and stated that it was the Gang of Four who had been guilty of adopting the ideology of "landlords, counter-revolutionaries, and bad elements as well as old and new bourgeois elements."[79] There was no serious attempt to relate class analysis to social relations of production or to identifiable differences in life-style. The only criterion was the dichotomy between the current line and the identified enemy.

Ye Jianying, the former marshal of the People's Liberation Army (who in 1979 was chairman of the Standing Committee of the Fifth National People's Congress and a member of the Politburo of the 11th Central Committee of the CCP), provided the most cogent statement of contemporary views about classes in his national day address:

> It is necessary to make a scientific analysis—one which conforms to objective reality—of the internal class situation and class struggle after the establishment of the socialist system and adopt correct policies and measures accordingly. Class struggle still exists to a certain extent after the exploiters in our country no longer exist as classes. While rejecting the view that class struggle no longer exists, we must oppose the view that magnifies it, to say nothing of creating so-called class struggles out of the void. We must strictly distinguish between the two different types of contradictions and *never mistake contradictions among the people for those with the enemy*, still less conduct inner-Party struggle the way we fight the enemy. This is the only way to maintain a social and political situation characterized by stability and unity.[80]

There is certainly no scientific analysis of classes here; Ye simply promulgated a new Party line. Having concluded that dialectical materialism is "the only true science," the Party divided society into friends and enemies and called it scientific class analysis. If anything, the speech was a public self-criticism for the entire Party's role in the Cultural Revolution. In the most important statement on the first thirty years of its history, the Chinese Communist Party reduced Marxist class analysis to the categorization of the Chinese people into two camps based on a dogmatic epistemology. The only reference to class analysis (which *should* relate the ownership of the means of production to life-style, economic position, and common ideas and interests) occurred in one short paragraph in the introduction by Ye. He said that classes in China were composed of "the state owned sector under the ownership of the whole people (*quanmin suoyouzhi*); the collectively owned sector (*jiti suoyouzhi*), including the rural people's communes and various enterprises in towns and cities; and the individual economy (*geti jingji*), practiced on a limited scale by urban and rural working people."[81]

Ye makes no mention of the position of the intellectual in the PRC's class structure. The relationship of Party and state cadre to classes is not considered. The division between mental and manual, or productive and unproductive, labor is ignored. Ye's speech is an example of apology clothed in the rhetoric of a party that appears to have lost its ability to do more than maintain its own ruling authority. Nonetheless, Xu Dixin, one of China's foremost political economists in the 1950s, cited the speech as accurately describing classes in China as well as "clearly characterizing class struggle."[82]

It is as though the entire subject of class analysis has become taboo in China. In 1982, between the archives of the East Asian Collection of the Hoover Institution of War, Revolution, and Peace and the collection of Chinese-language materials at the Universities Services Center in Hong Kong, no books published after 1975 in China were available that discuss class analysis in China. One would think that more sources could be located by a visit to a major library in China. However, that is not the case. At the library of Beijing University between October 1982 and May 1983 there was a two-inch empty gap in the card catalogue in the spaces where one should find listings on "Class," "Class Struggle," or "Class Analysis." The same is true of the collections at the Shanghai Municipal Library and the Nanjing University Library. Only one title was still listed in any of the catalogues—almost lost in the open space where catalogue cards had apparently been removed.

This book, a restricted publication classified "for internal distribution only" (*nei bu*), is an analysis of Soviet theories of class in socialist societies.[83] It was edited and published by the Chinese Academy of Social Sciences in 1980 as a Marxist analysis of classes in socialist society applicable to China.[84] Perhaps its publication represents an attempt by Chinese social scientists to come to grips with the paucity of class analysis and theory in their country.

The theoretical discussions in the book emphasize that there will necessarily be a transition period from capitalism through socialism to communism. During the stages of this transition—and no one can say how long it will last—a socialist state must be willing to accommodate three types of economic differences: (1) a socialist economy of collective ownership or ownership by the whole people, (2) a small-commodity economy, and (3) a capitalist economy that may be residual or may be engendered by the small-commodity economy.[85] The coexistence of these three forms of economy will, of course, produce contradictory relations in society; some of these will be antagonistic, but most will be nonantagonistic.

The only antagonistic relations are those between capitalists (including new capitalist owners engendered by a small-commodity economy) and socialist workers and peasants.[86] This is true in a socialist state ruled by a communist party even long after the political power of capitalists is toppled.[87] Nonantagonistic relations exist not only between paired sets of workers in different classes but also between those in the same class. For instance, among industrial workers we find two (socialist) classes: those employed in collectively owned industry and those employed in state-owned industry. These classes may have competing and contradictory interests because of the allocation of resources in the socialist state. However, because all of the workers are part-owners of the state-owned industries, their contradictory interests are nonantagonistic. The conflicts that may arise (rural versus urban industry, heavy versus light industry, oil versus coal industry) are sectoral, not class, conflicts.

Because a socialist economy is planned, there are other sets of competing nonantagonistic interests in the society, such as the allocation of resources in the economy between industry and agriculture or national defense. This situation creates further contradictions in interest between workers and peasants, but still these contradictions are nonantagonistic. Among peasants, the book distinguishes two classes: those on state-owned farms and those on collectively owned farms. Still, no antagonistic interests exist between them despite conflicting interests. Such conflicts are those that occur in any socialist enterprise—whether to concentrate on planned production or commodity production that supports the individual economy.[88]

Because of the coexistence of economic forms and the lack of political power for capitalists, the book suggests that *in a socialist society class is related to the scarcity of wealth, the distribution of wealth, and the social organization of labor.*[89] All workers, both manual and mental (including Party cadre, clerks, and intellectuals), constitute a single class. Those who own the means of production collectively are a stratum of the working class, and the employees of state institutions are another stratum of the working class. Of course, there can be no antagonistic relations between these strata, since those who own or work in collectively owned enterprises also are part-owners of the state-owned enterprises.[90] Interests may differ—for instance, because peasants are at the same time in different categories: they may be engaged in the individual economy while concurrently they are employed on a state farm—but it is plain that the thrust of the analysis is toward demonstrating the existence of a unitary social class with strata.[91]

The analysis in the book is compatible with Stalin's 1936 speech on classes in socialist society and with Mao's essay, "On the Correct Handling of Contradictions among the People"; it must be very easy for social scientists at the Chinese Academy of Social Sciences to accept. The Soviets analyze socialist society in terms of its own economic components: (1) the productive realm composed of a state-operated economy, a cooperative economy, a capitalist economy, and an individual economy; (2) the nonproductive sectors of national defense, administration and management, social welfare, and culture; and (3) the household economy of individual laborers and small service or cooperative producers. There is identifiable progress toward a communist state in the Soviet Union even though individual producers continue to exist. Soviet society comprises a single class of workers led by a ruling stratum.[92]

Published Chinese analyses of class, on the other hand, remain ideologies.[93] The Party has placed limitations on class analysis by turning its official epistemology into a program for action that cleaves society into opposing parts and then provides a platform from which to attack the "offending" section of itself.[94]

The constitution adopted by the Twelfth Congress of the CCP contains no class analysis. It states, almost quoting Ye Jianying's national day speech, that "after the elimination of the exploiting classes as such, most of the contradictions of Chinese society do not have the nature of class struggle, and class struggle is no longer the principal contradiction."[95] The most important task is to distinguish correctly "contradictions between the enemy and ourselves and those among the people."[96]

An article in the Beijing daily newspaper *Guangming Ribao* provides an important analytical commentary on class composition based on the new constitution. All workers, manual and mental, are categorized as members of the working class; therefore no antagonistic relations may exist between intellectuals and other members of Chinese society.[97] This assessment, which parallels that contained in the *nei bu* Soviet analysis of classes, follows the thrust of a commentary from a 1979 Shanghai newspaper.[98]

According to the Shanghai commentary, intellectuals have class interests that are intrinsically linked to the class to which they attach themselves through their work. Because intellectuals may be found in the countryside, working in agricultural units; in the cities, employed in state institutions; or employed in the collective economy, they are members of classes that have mutually nonantagonistic relations. Mental labor, like manual labor, is considered to be work of a continuous nature; therefore intellectuals are a part of "the people." The idea of a single, unified class of workers has begun to emerge in China.

One month after the adoption of the new Party constitution, the People's Liberation Army (PLA) newspaper, *Jiefangjun Bao*, published an article that completely redefined class in China.[99] In its discussion of the new constitution, the PLA paper concluded that "the ideologies of exploiting classes [capitalism] still represented a serious threat to China."[100] To overcome this threat, the people of China must strike out at "hostile elements" in a "kind of class struggle."[101] An article in the Party journal *Hong Qi*, printed before the new constitution was adopted, agreed that the new enemy classes of China include (1) "new exploiters engaged in graft, speculation, swindling, smuggling, who steal state and economic property"; (2) "criminals who seriously undermine the social order"; (3) "counter-revolutionaries and enemy agents"; and (4) "a very small number of old exploiters such as former landlords and rich peasants in rural areas who have not reformed, and unreformed reactionary capitalists in urban areas."[102]

Here it is obvious that the Party has totally revised the meaning of class to counter criminal acts. Because the revision followed criticism by the Socialist Democracy Movement, it is probably a means to deflect popular criticism of corruption and excesses on the part of Party cadre. An economic and social relationship (class) was confused with a moral and legal issue. The elimination of social distinctions lost importance for Party theorists, and serious class distinctions were declared to be absent in China (although they existed in Hong Kong, Macao, and Taiwan).[103] New contradictions in society, primarily the moral and legal problems involved in the abuse of a public office, were seen as influences that crept in from capitalist areas to corrupt socialists. Meanwhile, the working class was told to defer any benefits and privileges for itself and to devote itself to "its arduous and historical mission with regard to the future of the socialist cause."[104] At the same time, an extensive campaign was conducted in the Chinese press between September 1982 and January 1983 which sought to excise corruption from the administration of Chinese society.

To understand why this redefinition came about, the reader must understand that the Party, in the eyes of Chinese society, had begun to transform itself into the major abuser of privilege. The Party was what Milovan Djilas had called the "new class." Before and just after the new Party constitution there came a rectification campaign that was paralleled only by the "*san fan yun dong*" (three anti's) campaign of 1951–1952, when the Party eliminated many of its corrupt cadre.[105] However, to what extent were these allegations supported by evidence?

The next chapter discusses the image of the Party in popular literature. How was the Party and cadre privilege perceived by social commentators? Revolutionary writers try to show society realistically, pointing out its virtues and its evils. Art is attached to politics, but it criticizes the Party from the vantage point of the writer in the workplace. The treatment of cadres in this literature demonstrates the basis for the rectification campaign.

4

The Mass Line: Images of Class in Current Literature

To gain and retain the allegiance of intellectuals, traditionally Confucian scholars, has been the goal of Chinese rulers through the centuries.[1] The privileges of the Confucian scholar, as a member of a ruling class, were guaranteed by the imperial order in China. The imperial administrative system, primarily through its formal examinations, was a means to ensure that intellectuals adhered to orthodox thinking that supported dynastic rule.[2] At the same time, perhaps because of their strong Confucian moral training, intellectuals often spoke out against injustice and inequalities in government. Traditionally, they called for humanitarian change or reform of the state bureaucracy. Such criticism took different forms: petitions to the emperor, the preparation of philosophical tracts, and withdrawal from the system. A principal form of social criticism has been literature.

After the dynastic order crumbled, during the Republican period, the May Fourth Movement demonstrated that intellectuals still played a crucial role in reforming China. The May Fourth Movement takes its name from a demonstration in Beijing by professors and students on that date in 1919.[3] The demonstration was directed against the Chinese government's humiliation at the Versailles Peace Conference, at which the former German territory of Shandong was ceded to Japan. But events following China's defeat by Japan in 1894, especially the twenty-one demands calling for Japanese control of China (delivered in 1915), contributed to the intellectuals' ire.[4] The movement generally took on a broader meaning and is now used to refer to a period between 1917 and 1921 when there was an emphasis on Western liberalism, pragmatism, and utilitarianism over traditional Chinese ethics.[5] Marxism, socialism, and anarchism were introduced into China during this period.

The May Fourth Movement sought to liberalize Chinese society through intellectual and social reform. One means for this liberalization was the publication of literature written in vernacular style that could be read by persons who had no classical education. The new vernacular literature supported a general assertion of the movement that intellectuals, through literature, should provide a realistic and critical reflection of Chinese society in their art. The effect of the May Fourth Movement makes the study of literature a vehicle for the understanding of political and social phenomena in China.

THE RELATIONSHIP BETWEEN LITERATURE AND LIFE

Political criticism of the government in literature was the subject of fierce debate in 1919 and continued to be an explosive issue throughout the Anti-Japanese War and the Hundred Flowers and Anti-Rightist campaigns of 1956–1957.[6] Today, the CCP argues that literature should support the Party program, encourage socialist construction, and build China's socialist modernization.[7] However, others in and out of the Party argue in favor of critical literature.[8]

In its reassessment of the history of the CCP the Sixth Plenary Session, Eleventh Central Committee, affirmed that the debate over the nature and role of literature in China is still a fundamental issue confronting the CCP.[9] The resolution adopted by that session with regard to Party history points out that Mao Zedong's works on ideology, politics, and culture are "of tremendous significance even today."[10] The basic line offered by Mao on the question of culture is that while philosophy may interpret the world, the role of the Communist Party is to change the world.[11] Mao held that "any given culture is a reflection of the politics and economics of a given society, and the former in turn has a tremendous influence and effect upon the latter; economics is the base and politics the concentrated expression of economics. This is our fundamental view of the relation of culture to politics and economics and of the relation of politics to economics."[12]

Mao believed that literature, as a form of culture, reflected the struggles among classes and the relations of classes to the means of production. He also believed that the content of literature had a political application—as a tool for either critical interpretation or for the Party's use in building its own political base with propaganda.[13] In this regard Mao's views are in agreement with some of the principal Soviet Marxist theorists on art and literature. Anatoly V. Lunacharsky (1873–1933), the first People's Commisar of Education in the Soviet Republic, held much the same view: "artistic works depend directly upon the forms of production in a society. . . . A work of literature always reflects, whether consciously or unconsciously, the psychology of the class it represents."[14] Leon Trotsky made similar arguments. He believed that while economics is the base for politics, politics and literature, as they build socialism, influence economics.[15]

In his May 2, 1942 introduction to the Forum on Literature and Art at the guerrilla base in Yanan, Mao told his audience that literature may be used both to "extol and expose."[16] But in Mao's view literature should extol the virtues of the masses, the Party, and the anti-Japanese struggle while it exposes and criticizes enemies and those not participating actively in the war of resistance. The most telling question Mao asked was, "Literature and art for whom?"[17] Lunacharsky asked similar questions in his "Theses on the Problems of Marxist Criticism." Lunacharsky believed that any literary piece that sided with the proletariat was good and any work that was judged to harm the proletariat was evil.[18]

By the conclusion of the Yanan conference on May 23, 1942, after some debate over whether criticism of the Party was permissible in literature, Mao acknowledged that literature and art should reflect life for the masses:

> In the last analysis, what is the source of all literature and art? Works of literature and art, as ideological forms, are products of the reflection in the human brain of the life of a given society. Revolutionary literature and art are the products of the reflection of the life of the people in the brains of revolutionary writers and artists. The life of the people is always a mine of raw materials for literature and art, materials in their natural form, materials that are crude, but most vital, rich and fundamental; they make all literature and art seem pallid by comparison; they provide literature and art with an inexhaustible source, their only source. They are the only source, for there can be no other.[19]

Mao's statement accepts only a material basis for artistic and literary creation. There is no room in his universe for imagination, truth, or beauty; individual personality and consciousness are meaningless. A person is human in a definite social setting that produces his or her class character. On this point, in the Marxist view, there may be no compromise, for to accept that things may be true because they correspond to a fundamental reality that transcends the perceived universe and experience negates Marxist materialism.

Mao tells us that literature is drawn from the perceptions of the people, from their lives, and therefore corresponds with the material world. He says that ideals in literature are worthwhile to the extent that they present goals that serve the communist cause:

> Life as reflected in works of literature and art can and ought to be on a higher plane, more intense, more typical, nearer the ideal and therefore more universal than actual everyday life. Revolutionary literature and art should create a variety of characters out of real life and help the masses to propel history forward.[20]

The didactic nature of literature is acknowledged by Mao, but he insisted that the literary craft be used for a single purpose: to support the Party. Because he viewed literature as always the literature of a class, Mao applied the same epistemology to literature that he used in place of political economy in class analysis: the bifurcation of the members of society into enemy or friend.

There remains a constant tension between two opposing forces in the literary and political fields: those who maintain that true literature and art have a critical function beyond the moralizing and instructional function, and those who maintain that the major role of literature should be to support the Party and socialist construction. This tension surfaced during the course of the May 1982 Forum on Literature and Art when editorials in Chinese newspapers reminded artists and writers to obey the CCP and ensure that their work supported the Party.[21] Meanwhile, popular debate among writers and artists apparently rejected the dictum that art must serve the Party. Attendees at the conference supported the role of the author as a social critic with a responsibility to reflect popular opinion.[22] The Party, however, makes it quite clear that its policy dictates that literature and art serve the principles of socialism and support Party doctrine; it emphasized these points in 1985.[23]

The Party's policy has not wavered, for these are much the same points made by Hu Yaobang at a 1980 forum on scriptwriting.[24]

The abstraction of "popular opinion" is difficult to make when dealing with a Marxist-Leninist party. If the "masses" have not achieved a clear consciousness of themselves as a class, in the way that the Communist Party finds acceptable, the opinions of the masses may be rejected. People may simply be accused by the Party of laboring under the spell of "false-consciousness." Therefore a vanguard party may implement a program in spite of opposition.

Artists and writers, in their attempt to remain true to their craft and reflect popular opinion, publish works that suggest a different view of classes and the social structure than that offered by the Communist Party. In literature, Party officials are criticized for being able to secure special privilege because of Party membership, for using their position to advance personal or family interests, for corruption, and for a complacent bureaucratic attitude.[25] To the extent that such criticism is directed at the CCP as a whole, the criticism must be analyzed to see if it reflects differences attributable to being of a different social class. What is the basis for stratification in Chinese society? Do Party members or their offspring have different educational opportunities? Do they live a different life-style?

PEOPLE'S LITERATURE: THE CHOICE OF A JOURNAL

Renmin Wenxue is the major national literary journal in China. It provides a means to analyze the nature of class relations and social schisms as reflected in literature. It is an official publication operated under the supervision of the Chinese Communist Party. Authors published in it are supportive of the communist cause (although they are not necessarily Party members). The literature in the journal is not "counterrevolutionary" in nature.[26] It is literature that endeavors to support the Party while also providing loyal but critical comments on the Party's faults. Writers who publish in the journal see themselves acting as the voice of the masses of workers and peasants, reflecting mass views in China.[27]

Between January 1976 and December 1981 *Renmin Wenxue* published approximately 325 short stories in 72 issues. This five-year period is particularly worthy of study because it spans (1) the end of the

Cultural Revolution, incorporating some literature advocating the line of Jiang Qing and her associates; (2) the advent of literature of "wounds and exposure," the period when the Party reassessed its own history; and (3) the Socialist Democracy Movement, when the very basis of Party legitimacy was questioned (the literature of the movement is covered in the next chapter).[28] This period is a watershed for current domestic political policy in China.

Clearly, these 325 short stories were too much material to incorporate in a section of this study. Therefore a refined approach to the literature is needed.[29] First, this chapter reviews the discussion revolving around the case of Hu Feng, a literary figure in the postrevolutionary period. Next, the chapter reviews what is generally considered to be one of the most significant short stories published during the Hundred Flowers Campaign. The reaction to this story by Party authorities led to a general criticism of Chinese authors for their views on the role of literature during the Anti-Rightist Campaign. Finally, the chapter explores the stories from *Renmin Wenxue*, comparing the issues in the stories with points developed by the author during discussions with workers and students in China.

Hu Feng

Hu Feng was one of the directors of *Renmin Wenxue* in 1954. Party policies toward intellectuals relaxed in 1953, but within a year measures were instituted to regiment intellectuals. The climax of this process was a campaign against Hu.[30] Ever critical of the Party's role in the suppression of literary creativity, Hu referred to party authorities as "*guan men*" (the Mandarins), accusing the CCP of "warlord domination of the literary world."[31] The standard of analysis for authors in China was to ensure that literature served the Party. Remember, Mao said,

> our stand is that of the proletariat and of the masses. For members of the Communist party this means keeping to the stand of the Party, keeping to Party spirit and Party policy. Are there any literary and art workers who are still mistaken or not clear in their understanding of this problem? I think there are. Many of our comrades have frequently departed from the correct stand.[32]

Hu, however, steadfastly insisted that literature should be skeptical of authority (even that of the Party) and critical of social problems:

> True literature and art should duly reflect the demands of the time and speak for the people. . . . In literature and art productions there must be scathing criticism of the dark living conditions of an undemocratic social structure, the heritage of a nation with a history of a several thousand years. The productions should sincerely sympathize with the sufferings of the working people and at the same time play up their strength and power.[33]

Hu's view of socialist realism differed from the aesthetic canon adopted by the Party at Yanan. The orthodox Party doctrine, like Soviet aesthetics, insisted that art depict life as the Party says it should be.[34] Hu Feng, in contrast, sought a critical realism in his work that pointed to the evils in socialist society.[35]

The Hu Feng case provides an appreciation for the depth of emotion in artists and writers in China who insist that literary truth and realism in art are the most important in reflecting life. Writers heard Mao instruct that the "objective realities of class struggle determine our thoughts and feelings."[36] The writers were told to "study the various classes in society, their mutual relations and respective conditions, their physiognomy and their psychology," and to reflect these relations in literature.[37] Then, when the writers did so, faithful to the truth of their art—screaming for these "Mandarins" of Party cadre to correct social problems—they were severely criticized and attacked for subjective idealism. This rending struggle in the published media reflects a deeper struggle between the masses and the Party, making the literary journal as alive as a village marketplace.

The sharp intrusion of the Party into the world of the intellectual, exemplified in the case of Hu Feng, illustrates the basis for their opposition to the Party. Artists feel the anguish of being torn between a party and an ideology that they support, accepting its messianic promise, and a schism between that Party and the populace over issues regarding CCP cadre privilege. The apparent inability of the Party to live up to its own promise stimulates critical literature. What makes the entire conflict so fascinating to watch is that it takes place in the public arena. An official journal, managed by professional cadre, publishes stories by artists loyal to the Party but critical of its style. Meanwhile these artists, falling back on Mao's insistence at Yanan that artists and literary workers go out among the people to reflect their views, use their art to demand (often through the deepest of metaphor) that the Party be true to its doctrine, its theory, and its promise.

Wang Meng

Examination of a story in *Renmin Wenxue* by Wang Meng, from the period of the Anti-Rightist Campaign, is important to this study because the story proved to be one of the foremost examples of the use of fiction in open criticism of Party activities.[38] When *Renmin Wenxue* published the short story in 1956, Mao Zedong had just called for the Party to "let one hundred flowers bloom and one hundred schools of thought contend."[39] In response to this call Wang Meng published his short story, "A New Young Man Arrives at the Organization Department." In the story, Lin Chen, a new Party member, young and enthusiastic, arrives at his first assignment to work in the Party organization department of a factory. But Lin's idealism turns into a fight against privilege, inefficiency and incompetence. From the time of his arrival at the factory Lin is confronted with immediate privilege—and these privileges, as they are proffered, fly in the face of how Lin believes a Party member should be treated. Whereas all of the workers must sign in at the factory, Lin is allowed to enter without such formalities because he is going to work in the Party organization department. This was a small privilege that only relieved a minor inconvenience. Nonetheless, it was a privilege afforded only the Party cadre and it formed Lin's initial impression of the factory's Party leader. Lin also realized that he was expected by the workers to seek such privilege.

When Lin met his senior supervisor in the organization department, he was shocked anew. The supervisor suggested that as a new man in the factory Lin might be lonely; perhaps a "lady friend" selected from among the workers of the factory may make him more comfortable. Both the Party constitution and the norms of behavior taught at Party schools forbade such behavior. The Communist Party cadre is to be the model of the new China. A cadre's behavior should be above reproach at all times. But Lin found that the senior cadre at the factory, his first-line leader, implied that it is easier to find a "lady friend" because of status in the Party organization department.

Wang Meng's suggestion that Communist Party cadre routinely use their positions for personal advantage, and encourage subordinates to do the same, went beyond veiled criticism of the Party. Before the end of the story, through using Lin Chen as mouthpiece, Wang attacked the Party for bureaucracy, inefficiency, and a concern for satisfying self-interest at the expense of duty. Because he took these views, Wang was severely criticized in the Anti-Rightist Campaign. Although he later recanted and made a self-criticism, he had effectively charged that the Party had replaced the bourgeoisie as a privileged elite in China.[40]

Wang Meng discussed the disillusionment of young people with the ideals of the Party; he showed the frustrations of attempts to lead a life of *praxis*.[41] He condemned Party bureaucrats, high officials, and ordinary workers for inertia.[42] The Party, its competence challenged from within, was further frightened by uprisings that questioned Communist Party legitimacy in Hungary and Poland (much as it was in 1978–1979). The CCP response was a campaign that blighted literary criticism for two decades, until after the Cultural Revolution.[43] After the death of Mao Zedong, Wang Meng, like many other writers of the period, resumed his criticism of the Party. In examining the post-Mao period we will first review stories by some of the writers who were attacked during the Anti-Rightist Campaign.

Post-Mao Literature

The literature published in *Renmin Wenxue* between 1976 and 1982 has two distinct characteristics. The stories idealize the Marxist vision of a classless society, presenting a romantic vision of the Communist Party and its cadre as ''newly made beings'' of high moral virtue. At the same time, having seen or been subjected to the reprisals of the Anti-Rightist Campaign, the authors are more subtle in their criticism than those of the earlier period.[44]

Party heroes are most often depicted as more than human, without any faults or individualistic feelings. They derive emotional fulfillment from their responsibilities to the Party. The future, despite any mistakes other cadres may have made or any problems created by Party policy, will always be better. Ru Zhijuan, for example, in his story of the sacrifices of peasants in northern China to help achieve the 1949 revolution, criticizes the way that the same enthusiastic support of the peasants was wasted by the misguided Party policies of the Great Leap Forward.[45] Despite the errors in policy, the simple peasant heroes remain committed to the Party and its local representatives—confident that any new political mass movement will be correct and legitimate.

In this literature abuses by Party cadre and even high Party officials are viewed only as problems in "workstyle" (*zuofeng*) or as deficiencies in "consciousness" (*renshi*) that can be corrected if the cadres are enlightened through reeducation or criticism and if they adopt a correct workstyle once their consciousness is raised.

Another author, Bai Hua, who at the time of publication was an officer in the army's cultural and propaganda apparatus, published a story that dealt with the corruption of senior military officers.[46] He sought to demonstrate in his tale how a network of corruption extended throughout the military, involving even the families of the officers. His moral, however, adhered to the Party line: a "genuine" acceptance of Party goals can correct deficiencies in workstyle, eliminating corruption.

After the CCP Eleventh Central Committee's Third Plenum there was a new period of open debate and criticism of the Party which coincided with the activity in the Socialist Democracy Movement during spring 1979.[47] However, the Beijing Spring movement was suppressed in short order and Party authority over the literary field was reestablished.[48]

Deng Xiaoping, in his 1979 speech to the Fourth Congress of Chinese Writers and Artists on October 30, 1979, signaled clearly that literature and art must support Party programs. Literature and art were to be "guided by the correct principles for creative work," meaning that while different forms and styles of expression were acceptable, the content of the work was to "serve . . . the workers, peasants and soldiers."[49] These principles were affirmed in a 1985 *Red Flag* article, which states that artists are free only to "find ways and means of making socialist literature and art flourish."[50]

Through a series of policy statements made by officials, writers were told to support the Party line:

> Restudying today the "Talks at the Yanan Forum on Literature and Art," we profoundly feel that although many of Comrade Mao Zedong's expositions were most applicable to the historical conditions of that time, the basic ideology running through the work is the incisive analysis of historical materialism, and that is the demand posed on revolutionary literature and art work by the application of the basic principles of historical materialism.[51]

As one might expect from an official Party journal, the literature in *Renmin Wenxue* rarely analyzes the structure of the social order or the problems inherent in a communist system.[52] Generally, literature and art works fail to distinguish between the CCP, the state, and the socialist system. The works criticize factions, groups, or programs in a manner acceptable to the Party; but there is no reflection on the underlying system that may have caused the problems.[53] Considering the attacks by the Party on writers during the mid-1950s and the imprisonment of social critics in 1979, the authors demonstrate considerable courage by publishing as they have. Their muted criticism, even in metaphor, risks Party wrath.

The interpretive analysis in this chapter seeks to probe deeper into the short stories to note the deficiencies inherent in the political organization of Chinese society that one can infer from the problems expressed in literature.[54] The objective of this analysis is to display institutionalized, systemic problems in the political order that are symptomatic of the relationship to the means of production that cadre and high officials enjoy.

The Short Stories

''*Zhuren*.'' One story that typifies the genre of the literature published in *Renmin Wenxue* is Zhou Yongnian's ''Zhuren'' (Master), published when the Gang of Four was at the height of its power.[55] ''Zhuren'' takes place at the East Wind Foodstuffs Factory, where the Workers' Management Committee holds a worksite meeting to consider whether to stop the production of salt soda water in favor of producing sweet soda water. The Workers' Committee Director, Tao Zhenqing, argues that the production of salt soda water should continue, whereas one staff economist wants to shift to the product that will sell best and earn the most income—sweet soda water. The economist is portrayed as an antagonist in the story whose political judgment is faulty for two reasons: first, during the Cultural Revolution he never engaged in physical labor; therefore he never received a good proletarian education. Second, he considers only profit when making decisions, not what is good for the industries supplied by the plant. Tao believes that earnings should not be a consideration; salt soda water, according to him, is good for the workers' bodies and will help them to be healthier so that they can produce more for the state. This argument over what type of soda water to produce parallels the struggle between the capitalist line and the communist line. It is a story of good or evil, friend or foe.

On the surface the story supports the correct communist line, criticizing excessive worry about profit. However, the title contains a subtle condemnation of the "good" Workers' Committee Director Tao.

The ideographs for *zhuren* mean master or owner. Whereas on the surface the story supports the line of the Gang of Four, the double meaning in the title actually criticizes the system of revolutionary committees in enterprises as undemocratic. The workers and the economist, who should be the "masters" as the real owners of the means of production, would like to run a more profitable business. However, the manager—who is, of course, a Party member—dictates what policy should be followed. The workers at the factory have no opportunity for self-determination. They may be the legal owners of the means of production, but the Party dictates to the workers how production should be organized and what is produced—the Party representative is the "Master."

"*Ren-Yao zhijian.*" The same accusation that the *real* master of a socialist enterprise is the Party chief, not the workers who legally own the means of production, is made by Liu Binyan in the story "Between Human and Demon." The story by Liu, available in English translation, tells of rebellious factions in Heilongjiang, covering a twenty-five-year period.[56] The story's opening evokes images of a Communist Party bureaucracy that is gradually alienated from the peasants. "Between Human and Demon" opens with a description of a courtyard outside Party headquarters that was once a popular gathering place in a rural Heilongjiang county seat:

> For years or so after land reform, when people came here on market days . . . , they would look in on cadres who had been . . . stationed in their villages to talk things over. But as time wore on, the wall around the courtyard seem to grow higher and thicker until it took on a secretive and awe-inspiring look. People passing by would seldom pop their heads in to look about. By the early sixties [when there was a famine] the sweet enticing smell of meat, oil, and steamed bread would frequently assail the nostrils of passers-by, some of whom would crack bitter smiles, grumbling: "Well, they're doing quite well, this group of officials."[57]

Throughout the story Liu makes it clear that regardless of the official Party line on classes and social stratification, a different system was practiced. In the story ranking highest in the social sphere are Party secretaries and standing committee members; next in importance are members of the armed forces; next under them are members of local Party organization departments; below them are administrators who controlled personnel, finance, and labor; finally, people who controlled such commodities as beer, baked goods, and candies were accorded special privilege in the social order.

Liu Binyan closes the story on a poignant note: he does not see an appreciable difference between stratification in post-Mao China and during the Cultural Revolution. When new calls for democracy came from college campuses in 1986-1987, Liu was one of the three intellectuals disciplined by the Party as an example to others.

''*Xixian yishi.*'' In ''An Anecdote from the Western Front,'' author Xu Huaizhong's intent is to praise the contributions of a squad of women soldiers during China's punitive invasion of Vietnam in 1979.[58] In the story Xu excuses the Party's errors during the Cultural Revolution and the period when the Gang of Four was in power. He compares the death of martyrs on the battlefield to those who died from Cultural Revolution excesses. The story discusses how special privilege for cadre extends into the army. Xu's protagonist is a female soldier who, although the daughter of a high-ranking cadre, was still doing her duty and going to the front. She had wholly embraced the ''communist spirit,'' and sought no special privileges.[59] Xu makes it clear that the ''back door'' of special privilege through family connections continues unchecked in the military; however, his heroine did not take advantage of this route.

Jiang Zilong. Jiang, an author who was responsible for the development of a character that became the paradigmatic hero of the Four Modernizations, was born in 1941 in an agricultural village in Hebei Province. Jiang became a worker in a Tianjin electrical equipment plant in 1958. He entered the People's Liberation Army in 1960 and returned to the same plant after his discharge in 1965. During the Cultural Revolution he held various leadership positions in workers' committees through 1971, when he joined the Chinese Communist Party.

In ''Commentary on a Shovel,'' Jiang Zilong tells of a brigade Party secretary whose life revolves around a shovel.[60] As a child she was named ''Sister Shovel'' (*Tiexian sao*) after having been saved from a flood by clinging to a spade. Thus she is the prototypical peasant heroine whose life is inextricably tied to one of the primary tools of agricultural production. The shovel also becomes a symbol of the spirit of the Communist Revolution and the fight against capitalistic profit motivation. Sister Shovel once used it to block the way of a truck carrying black market goods to market during the period when Liu Shaoqi advocated the "three freedoms and one contract" policy (*san zi yi bao*, extending agricultural plots for private use, increasing the number of enterprises responsible for their own profits and losses, and fixing output quotas on the basis of individual households).[61]

These very policies are those advocated by Deng Xiaoping, Zhao Ziyang, and the current leadership, but during the Gang of Four and Cultural Revolution periods the policies were attacked as following the capitalist road. In "Commentary on a Shovel," Jiang Zilong associates these policies with the pursuit of self-interest and, therefore, with corruption. In subsequent stories he glorifies *san zi yi bao* as the salvation of China's economy and the Party's mandate with the populace.

Through the character of Chang Chaobai, a county Party committee secretary, Jiang points out the emptiness of literary and artistic production during the Cultural Revolution by calling Cultural Revolution plays and poetry *hua zhong qu chong* (trying to please the masses with claptrap). Jiang is conscious of the depth of the split between the masses and the Party precipitated by the overemphasis on political form during the 1966–1976 period. Through Chang Chaobai, Jiang calls the policies "attending to trifles at the expense of essentials" (*she ben qiu mo*). The "trifle" to which Chang refers is the requirement that the proper political line be reflected in every medium; the essentials being ignored are the livelihood of the populace and the ability of workers to control their workplace.

The story proceeds to debate the concept of "bourgeois right" while encouraging the reader to engage in productive work instead of political study.[62] Sister Shovel finally sides with policies that would mitigate the overemphasis on ideological purity, advocating improvement in the living standards of the masses. The moral of this story is that the Party must provide leadership for the people, but it must also be responsive to the needs of the masses or become alienated from them.[63]

In contrast to "Commentary on a Shovel" in which Jiang Zilong chronicles the metamorphosis of a new Party line, his story "A Day in the Life of the Electrical Equipment Bureau Chief" creates a new role model for cadres while praising post-Mao policies.[64] The story encourages high levels of production but attacks profits. Consider this

Orwellian quote from Jiang: "the capitalist line is to speak of high profit and high production levels but to produce at a low level."[65] Thus failing to meet socialist production quotas is associated, according to the Party line, with capitalism. Here capitalism is not attacked as a system of ownership of the means of production but as a label for what is considered to be any form of anti-Party behavior. The bifurcation of behavior into categories of "friend" or "enemy" is reflected in such slogans.

In the story higher-level cadre prove unwilling to speak to or engage in debate with lower-level cadre. Their relationships resemble those in a wartime military chain of command rather than in a workplace. Only the obedience by lower-ranking cadre of orders issued from above is permitted. Of all the cadre, only one assistant director is willing to joke and speak freely with lower-level cadre. The director does not demonstrate even a casual interest in his workers or staff. Nonetheless, the director always has a special car and driver at his disposal. Although this car is collective property, the vehicle and the driver are controlled by the director.

In the short story "A Factory Secretary's Diary," Jiang speaks through the diary of a minor functionary who represents an institutional memory, a source of continuity at a factory between a series of directors who come and go at the whim of the ministries.[66] By virtue of his position as a secretary, the keeper of the diary has access to all of the workshops in the factory and is able to keep a record of the problems caused by cadre who do not perform their duties. The diary damns some of the "better" cadre with praise. Jiang tries to show that there are cadre with the interests of the workers in mind. However, the story demonstrates that the system of public ownership is flawed: the only way to accomplish anything seems to be through the use of the "back door" of personal relationships and influential friends. The deputy factory director's daughter expects a position at the factory because of her father's influence. She is ready to ignore state regulations that require her to go through a labor bureau and expects the secretary to do the same. When a worker needs to go to a funeral, the new factory director is able to use his influence to procure a car and driver.

The car, which should be available if the state system of ownership is working, is being used by the outgoing director. Through the influence of the new factory director another car is procured, but only by using the "back door." The message is that the Party is always correct, the system is good, even if some individual cadre do not live up to the ideals of the Party.

At a deeper level, the secretary is more than just a central character. He represents all of the Chinese people. They are stuck in their factories and in the fields with leaders imposed on them by higher authority. Sometimes the leaders are good, sometimes they are bad. The workers can help a good leader or hinder a bad leader. But like the secretary, they also have a vivid memory, a diary etched in their mind of what unfair policies were imposed on them in the past.

Qin Yanshen. In "A Record of Production Team Leader 'Stupid,' " Qin Yanshen criticizes the attitude that the Party is right under any circumstances.[67] To be a cadre, according to Qin, one need not be clever or skillful; one need only "arrange things right, obey orders, and give out plenty of work to others." In the story one production leader, nicknamed *An pai duizhang* ("The Arranger") because he farms out tasks to his subordinates, is challenged by a younger man. The Arranger immediately becomes ill when he agrees to change duties and perform manual labor in place of the challenger. "An pai duizhang" symbolizes the Party cadre who has become too familiar with the exercise of authority. He has forgotten his roots and ignored the basis of his authority, the willing cooperation of the peasants.

However, Qin does not go so far as to suggest that his hero, the "stupid" new team leader Zhao Chengping, is a success because he genuinely allows discussion among all members of the team, giving the peasants the opportunity for self-determination. Instead, Zhao (nicknamed "Stupid" by his predecessor because he lacks experience), does well because he listens to the Party and studied the works of Chairman Mao.

"*Tongzhi*." Liu Wu, in the recollection "Comrade," makes a telling criticism of the behavior and attitudes of cadres.[68] Liu points out that at one time the very term "cadre" had the connotation of a person attached to the Party as though it were a mother: eager to serve, thinking only of the people he or she leads. However, today the term is used with near derision to indicate a person who is attached to his or her position. The Party cadre is concerned only with the retention of position, privilege, and authority as paramount and gives no consideration to workstyle.

Fox Butterfield raises the same issue in his book, *China: Alive in the Bitter Sea*.[69] The institutionalization of the Party's authority over all walks of life makes the Party, in Butterfield's view, the only path for people who seek social advancement and noticeable improvements in their standard of living. This is a result of concentrated Party authority and has led to a generalized desire to ignore the tradition of selfless service. Many cadres are unwilling to make a commitment to take on leadership responsibilities.

"*Zhaohuan*." The theme of cadre privilege and influence is the central issue in Jiao Zuyao's short story, "The Summons."[70] A branch secretary of a city's Party committee has used his influence and position to ensure that his son is transferred from an agricultural commune in the countryside to a position in a factory in another city. Party branch secretary Wang was able to accomplish this by contacting an old cadre friend from the revolution who had also risen to the position of Party branch secretary. Events like this illustrate one of the more common complaints by Chinese workers and peasants: it is hard to return to an urban area after rustification. To be able to do so generally requires the assistance of someone of influence.

Party Secretary Wang's son is seriously injured in a fight with another factory worker, and Wang is summoned to the hospital in another city. The son dies, and everyone is convinced that because of Wang's position he will interfere in the administration of justice by ensuring that the culprit will be severely punished. On the trip to the other city Wang gets a special car. After his arrival he gets special treatment at the hospital. The parents of the culprit are ready to sacrifice their own son and expect that Wang will contact the judge to seal their son's fate. Wang, however, as a good cadre, takes no advantage of his position to interfere in the case. He allows the law to take its course.

The issue here should not be whether some old revolutionary cadres, represented by Wang, are good. The story implies that simply by virtue of membership in the Party any high-level cadre can use his or her position to circumvent established laws. If this is the case, Chinese policy at the national and local levels, the judicial system, and the administrative system of the state are only means to control the "little man," the average person. A cadre can circumvent all of these laws and gain access to special privilege for his or her entire family.[71]

"*Da nian chuyi*." One short story stands out among all of those discussed in this book. In "New Year's Day," Li Zhun pronounces judgment on the sixty-year history of the Chinese Communist Party through the character Ruan Xinyou, attempting to address the issue of whether the Party has alienated itself from the masses.[72]

This is a complicated story of symbolism and metaphor that is tied to the traditional Chinese calendar. The hero's surname, Ruan, is an ideograph that has no particular meaning and is a standard Chinese surname. However, it is a homophone for the ideograph that means "soft, plaible, weak, or easily moved or influenced." The hero's given name, Xinyou, is a combination of the ideographs for two of the ten heavenly stems and the twelve earthly branches that, when combined, form a sixty-year cycle based upon a combination of lunar and solar cycles.[73] Each year in the sixty-year cycle is represented by a two-ideograph combination. The ideographs *xin you* represent the years 1921 and 1981 in this century. The sixty-year cycle is further subdivided into five twelve-year cycles, and each twelve-year cycle is represented by an animal, to which certain characteristics are attributed. The year 1921, when Ruan Xinyou was born, is represented by the rooster (or cock), an animal that is alert and protective of its flock, always ready to defend, but which generally lacks intelligence. People born in the year of the cock are thought to be dedicated workers, but they tend to get involved beyond their abilities. They are hard to understand.

Because 1921 is Ruan Xinyou's birth year, which was also the year of the cock, and his sixtieth birthday is in 1981, another year of the cock, Ruan is convinced this will be an auspicious year for him. Ruan's convictions are reinforced by the fact that the ideograph for cock, *ji*, is a homophone for the ideograph *ji*, meaning "lucky, auspicious, or propitious." Therefore despite his position as a Party cadre in his village, Ruan Xinyou sets about to follow all of the traditional superstitions about the celebration of the new year in order to ensure good fortune.

Coincidentally, 1921 is also the year in which the Chinese Communist Party was formed. Thus the sixty-year cycle of Ruan Xinyou's life runs the same course as that of the Party and its first sixty years. As Ruan Xinyou faces these sixty years and sums up what he has amounted to, the CCP is also doing the same for the first sixty years of its history.[74] While the Party is engaged in revisionist history, our author, through Ruan Xinyou, tells us of a Party that has overreached the bounds of its own cadres' abilities. The cadre are undereducated, semiliterate, and remain under the influence of ancient superstition even though they advise others to ignore ancient custom. The Party has alienated the intellectuals of the country and relegated them to an insignificant position, ignoring their expertise and advice.

At one time Ruan Xinyou was a Party branch secretary in the Ruan Zhuang Brigade. However, he was later demoted to an assistant Party branch secretary and replaced by another man, one who is younger and without the revolutionary experience but who abides by the traditional superstitions of the countryside. In keeping with traditional superstition Ruan observes the new year rituals; buying firecrackers and preparing to set them off, and preparing New Year's couplets (*qun lian*, sayings that are displayed to bring luck in the new year). However, Ruan is only semiliterate; therefore he must go to the county cultural center to seek the help of an intellectual who formerly was rusticated to his brigade to have the couplets written.

The episode at the cultural center demonstrates the Party's continued reliance on intellectuals despite the way the CCP mistreated China's educated people; it also underscores the reliance of older CCP cadres on technocrats. Ruan wants a couplet written that refers only to the auspicious new year. But his old friend, the intellectual, advises him to exercise more political caution, suggesting a couplet that relates to the socialist construction of China and celebrates the future of the Party and the state. Ruan goes through the new year rituals—the dinner, the setting off of firecrackers—but he finds that they don't bring much pleasure. His son ignores him, most of the villagers ignore him, and he is convinced that this is because he is no longer Party branch secretary. He peeks at the scene in the new Party branch secretary's home, but he sees that the new secretary is also ignored. No one brings either of them the usual offerings and gifts; no one visits their houses. The Party is a marginal factor in people's lives—they are increasingly estranged from it. Ruan Xinyou and the Party must change their workstyle and their thinking if they are to have any influence in the nation.

ALIENATION FROM THE CCP

Political practice in China has deified the CCP leadership while weakening the influence of the populace over their own destinies. People are alienated from the control of production, from political power, and from economic power. Officials have become the masters of the country.[75]

One source of this alienation is the overcentralization of authority in the Party. The Party dominates society. However, the portrayal of official corruption in all of these stories never touched the roots of the structural problem that allows such practices to go unchecked: Party orthodoxy and the rigid subordination of Party members to a hierarchical relationship that allows no critical feedback. It is almost a military "crisis mentality" that is best characterized as the "Yanan Syndrome." This characterization is appropriate because it refers back to the common revolutionary experience of all of the senior Party cadre. Among the older cadre there seems to be the attitude that because "I suffered through the Long March and the 'Anti-Japanese War,' I deserve to become specially privileged (*te shu hua*)." Younger cadre, meanwhile, apparently seek higher office and Party membership as a means to secure access to privileges.[76]

In the story of women soldiers, family connections did not interfere in military duty. In the case of the injured son, family connections did not interfere in justice. However, the authors of these stories avoid mention of the numbers of people who do get special privilege because of Party position. The network of state and military guest houses, which sometimes are used for foreigners, is still in existence in China. Many of the workers at such guest houses are drawn from the relatives of senior army or Party cadre.

Jiang Zilong never questions whether problems at the factory may be the result of a rigid authority structure that locks out criticism. Qin Yanshen criticizes the attitude that the Party is right under all circumstances, but Qin does not go so far as to suggest that the roots of this attitude may be imbedded in the bedrock of "Democratic Centralism." The doctrine holds that

> the organizational form of the government will be democratic centralism, which is at once democratic and centralized, with the two seeming opposites of democracy and centralization united in a definite form. . . . On the one hand, the government we want must truly be representative of the popular will; it must have the support of the broad masses throughout the country and the people must be free to support it and have every opportunity to influence its policies. This is the meaning of democracy. On the other hand, the centralization of administrative power is also necessary, and once the policy measures demanded by the people are transmitted to their own elected government through their representative body, the government will carry them out and will cer-

tainly be able to do so smoothly, so long as it does not go against the people's will. This is the meaning of centralism.[77]

Unfortunately, relationships between cadre of different levels, and between cadres and the masses, are conducted more along rigid lines of authority: "Individual Party members are subordinate to the Party organization, the minority is subordinate to the majority, the lower Party organizations are subordinate to the higher Party organizations, and all the constituent organizations and members of the Party are subordinate to the National Congress and the Central Committee of the Party."[78]

The failure to differentiate among the Party, the state, and the socialist system in the literature reviewed in this chapter is symptomatic of the Party's hegemony over all forms of life in China: social, economic, administrative, and political. The next chapter explores this hegemony further. In the manner described by Stanislaw Ossowski in his analysis of the socialist system, the Party controls power relations, labor relations, and economic status.[79] These stories provide graphic examples of what Zygmunt Bauman, in reference to Poland, has called "partynomial" authority: dominance over all spheres of culture.[80] The CCP exercises control over basic-level enterprise and agricultural organizations; the CCP controls life in housing areas and the allocation of housing; the CCP influences who may receive a higher education; and the majority of officials in local, provincial, and national government are also Party members and must adhere to Party discipline:[81]

Every Party member, irrespective of position must be organized into a branch, cell, or other specific unit of the Party to participate in the regular activities of the Party organization and accept supervision by the masses inside the Party and outside the Party.[82]

Primary Party organizations are formed in factories, shops, schools, communes, cooperatives, farms, townships, towns, companies of the People's Liberation Army and other basic units where there are three or more Party members.[83]

The short stories from *Renmin Wenxue* provide fleeting images of privilege conferred by Party membership. They show people in the workplace who are increasingly alienated from the system but are impotent to change it. In China there is an experiential basis for the criticism in literature. The direct criticism of dissidents in the Socialist

Democracy Movement led to a campaign to eliminate Party corruption. The events surrounding the movement and the campaign offer opportunities to sample the way cadre could benefit from their position of control. The next chapter reviews the anticorruption campaign and the criticism by Chinese dissidents.

5

Economic Ownership: CCP Cadre and the Abuse of Power

The short story "Zhuren" by Zhou Yongnian suggested that the system of economic management in Chinese enterprises turned factory directors into the "masters" of the enterprise. Liu Binyan made the same accusation in "Between Human and Demon."[1] The Chinese dissidents who published the "Li Yizhe Manifesto" in 1974 used similar language to accuse careerist Party members of bastardizing the system of socialist ownership by "changing public into private" (*hua gong wei si*).[2] The Li Yizhe Manifesto charged that Party cadres "have completed the change from public servants of the people to masters of the people" by abusing the public trust and dipping into the public till.[3]

Although it is relatively easy to level such charges, it is more difficult to document them. Whether one calls these "masters" a "privileged stratum" or a "new class," one must first understand state planning and enterprise management in China in order to understand how the masters run the enterprise. Then, to substantiate the allegation, one must document cases of the seizure of public property for private use by cadre. Finally, one must determine whether the seizure of public property is an occurrence so common, and restricted to Party cadre, that the phenomenon can be characterized as symptomatic of a class.

After a summary of the enterprise management system in China, this chapter compares the charges of Chinese dissidents about cadre abuse of authority with cases made public during the 1981–1982 campaign to end the abuse of position by Party cadre. Although the reports of cadre abuse of privilege are widespread (there are 160 separate reports from all over China documented herein), one still cannot estimate with any precision how many cadre engage in such activities. A report based on an investigation by the Party's Central Discipline Inspection Commission uncovered a total of 192,000 "economic crimes in the course of a 16-month investigation which resulted in the expulsion from the CCP of 8,500 cadre."[4] The Party then had roughly 39 million members. The investigation reveals that the abuses are common enough to justify the charges leveled by the dissidents in the Socialist Democracy Movement.[5] Before reviewing specific cases, it is useful to introduce the concept of "economic ownership" as it applies to socialist society.

ECONOMIC OWNERSHIP

Legal title, guaranteed by state law, ensures that an individual or group of individuals (including the entire populace of a socialist or communist state) own property or specific means of production. Ownership, however, does not mean control—it does not necessarily translate into decision-making power over the property. One must examine the control exercised over that property or means of production to understand the concept of economic ownership. Those persons who have the power to dispose of commodities obtained from production, to regulate the work process and its results, and to assign the means of production for use are "economic owners."[6]

When we view the structural relationships in society from the perspective of the worker (or peasant) whose labor results in the production of commodities for the market, we must evaluate social relations of production with the criteria used by the worker:[7] Am I able to participate in decision-making in the enterprise? Have I any input to the state plan that levies quotas on my labor? What influence do I have on housing allocation, access to education, and job mobility? These questions concern relations of control and functional ownership in the society, not relations of ownership legitimated by possession of legal title to the means of production. To begin to understand how the citizens of a socialist state come to question the legitimacy of the ruling party—to label the party a "new class"—we must explore these questions.

In capitalist society the relationship between power and authority is subtly different from that in socialist society. Capitalist ownership confers power over the means of production, which confers the authority to make production decisions, to hire and fire workers, and to allocate resources.[8] Under socialism, the authority of the ruling Communist Party confers similar power on its cadre or on leaders they appoint, a power that has been characterized as *economic ownership* expressed in terms of the "real economic control of the means of production, i.e., the power to assign the means of production to given uses and to dispose of the products obtained."[9]

Certain managerial occupations—particularly when managers are also Party members—provide economic control of the means of production. According to E. O. Wright, this creates conditions that so closely approximate the conditions of ownership in a capitalist society that the distinction between capitalist owner and socialist manager is nearly indistinguishable.[10] Given the existence of a ruling communist party as the sole control structure, when the leaders of the economic system and the political system are also the leaders of the party (and that leadership has continual access to the control of the means of production), there exist conditions of economic ownership and relations of production that result in class subjugation.[11]

The following paragraphs briefly outline the lines of functional control in the general system of enterprise management and state planning in China. Regardless of whether workers or peasants have legal title to an enterprise, control of the enterprise is exercised through the senior cadre of its party committee.

State Planning and Enterprise Management

The general economic system in China is a mix of state-owned, collectively owned, and Chinese–foreign-owned joint venture enterprises. This enterprise system is supplemented by a limited network of individual tradesmen, craftsmen, and small service businessmen.[12] The economy is administratively directed by a central authority, the State Economic Commission of the State Council, which provides unified management under the general guidance of policies set by the CCP.[13] Jan S. Prybyla distinguishes between two general forms of Soviet-type socialist economies: (1) a highly centralized Stalinist economy, run like a multilevel corporation; and (2) a more decentralized model of "basic macroeconomic goal formulation and microeconomic output and input norm setting."[14] Different five-year plans (the base for economic management) in China have featured elements of both of these forms, depending on the policy guidelines set by the Party.

The five-year plans are used to manage the economy to provide for general production goals and establish economic development targets for the entire nation. The plans are intended to provide for balanced development among different sectors of the economy: agriculture, heavy industry, light industry, transportation, and so on. China's First Five Year Plan (FFYP) was modeled heavily on Soviet plans and depended on Soviet assistance.[15] Since the FFYP there has been "a history of stillborn, unfinished, unfinishable, and discarded wrecks" of plans.[16] Nonetheless, the State Economic Commission meets regularly to summarize the economic accomplishments of the previous year's economic plan and, in conjunction with the State Planning Commission, to establish the targets of the next year's plan. Adjustments to the five year plans are made at subsequent annual meetings or other routine meetings of the commission. Figures 1 and 2 provide the structure of the state council and its ministries and the lines of authority from ministry to enterprise.

The means for transmitting the plan to each enterprise and for adjusting targets for the plan is complicated. In some key industries, particularly those concerned with national defense, there are direct lines from the ministry to the individual enterprise. In other industries, especially those that are specific to geographical area, the lines of authority in the planning process may extend from the ministry through a local department to the enterprise. Alternatively, the lines of authority for the planning process may include the provincial bureau responsible for an enterprise with or without including the local authorities. In some cases national, provincial, local, and enterprise authorities are involved in the process.[17] "The late 1970's," according to one American economist, "found Chinese enterprises more rigidly controlled than in any other socialist country."[18]

Economic planning in China is further complicated by both institutional and geographic factors. Because the Chinese government conceals much of the available economic information at the central level, individual enterprises have very limited access to data.[19] Therefore enterprises have little information from outside sources on marketing, resources, transport, and demand on which to base their responses to the state plan. They must develop an enterprise plan in response to the state plan, but all of their targets come from the State Council and

Figure 1
The State Council and Its Ministries

National People's Congress (NPC)

Standing Committee of the (NPC)

Supreme People's Procurate | State Council | Supreme People's Court

Commissions

1. State Economic
2. State Planning
3. State Nationalities Affairs
4. State Physical Culture and Sports
5. State Family Planning
6. State Restructuring of the Economic System
7. State Scientific and Technological

Ministries (with economic responsibilities)

1. Agriculture, Animal Husbandry and Fishery
2. Aviation Industry
3. Chemical Industry
4. Civil Affairs
5. Coal Industry
6. Commerce
7. Communications
8. Electronics Industry
9. Finance
10. Foreign Economic and Trade Relations
11. Forestry
12. Geology and Minerals
13. Labor and Personnel
14. Light Industry
15. Machine Building Industry
16. Metallurgical Industry
17. National Defense
18. Ordnance Industry
19. Petroleum Industry
20. Posts and Telecommunications
21. Railways
22. Space Industry
23. Textile Industry
24. Urban and Rural Construction and Environmental Protection
25. Water Resources and Electric Power

SOURCE: Central Intelligence Agency, Evolution of the Commissions and Ministries of the State Council of the People's Republic of China, 1949-1982 (A Reference Aid) (CR 82-11388) (Washington, D.C., Library of Congress, 1982).

Figure 2
Ministry-to-Enterprise Lines of Authority

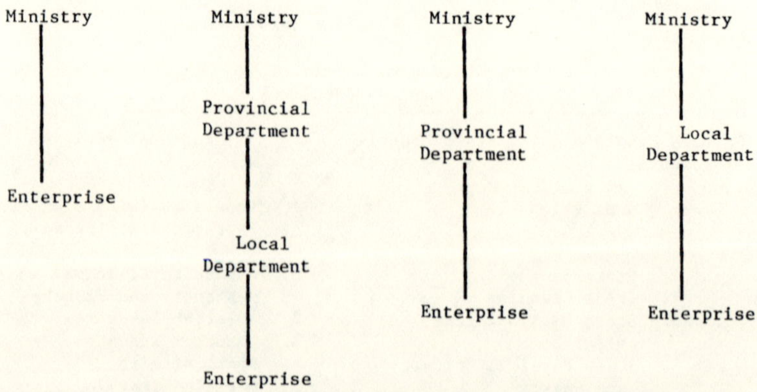

depend on materials provided by the state through state-directed transport. Although two top Chinese economists, Sun Yuefang (now deceased) and Xue Muqiao, have suggested that enterprises should be allowed more autonomy in determining their plan—using both market forces and central planning as considerations—the lack of data and an inadequate transportation infrastructure restrict the implementation of such suggestions.[20]

The Chinese state is simply unable to handle long-distance transport on a national scale, let alone intracity and short-distance transportation.[21] As a consequence, the use of open market forces to try to move goods effectively may not be practical, further constraining enterprise autonomy. Although 50 percent of China's approximately 72,000 agricultural production brigades are linked by highways, the roads are inadequate.[22] There is no centralized system of highway transport and no coordinated national highway system in the country.[23] The majority of available roads are either gravel or dirt, built with local materials by untrained labor. The flow of materials is interrupted by weather as well as by limited vehicle resources. China's railway system is well maintained and centralized, but about 40 percent of total rail volume is used to transport coal, the primary energy resource.[24] Were individual enterprises, particularly local commune enterprises, allowed to contract and transport their own materials and seek their own markets, the results could be chaotic. Xue Muqiao justifies continuing rigid state control for the following reasons:

> Corruption, waste, speculation and manipulation occur in some areas where strict control has not been exercised over commune and brigade industries. They [leading cadre] resort to gifts, wining and dining, and briberies to scramble for their own raw materials and market outlets. Since their raw materials, fuels, marketing and railroad transport have not been included in the state plan, they have to grease someone's palms to get anywhere. Some field personnel take these opportunities to line their own pockets and corrupt many staff and workers.[25]

Faced with the specter of the forms of corruption that revolutionaries sought to eliminate in the 1911 and 1949 revolutions, the CCP continues to rely on a planned economy. Market mechanisms are used only to adjust the plan, while the planning process seeks to unite the center with regions, districts, and localities.[26] Paradoxically, Chinese planners admit to having "managed the economy to death."[27]

The following paraphrases a description by factory managers at the Lanzhou Chemical Industries Corporation of the planning process in that enterprise. The corporation receives its production targets directly from the Ministry of Chemical Industry:

> Plans in our enterprise are drawn up annually in the 4th quarter of the year. Our targets come from the Ministry as part of State Council quotas. When the plant's Party committee gets the targets, it is discussed. Then the plan is presented to the plant management committee and to the workers and staff for discussion in committees. The factory plan is drawn up considering workers' suggestions regarding the previous year's production and then is sent back to the Ministry for acceptance. If the Ministry does not accept our factory plan they will send it back to us for revision. The plan tells us the quantity, quality, and cost relationships of our product. It will specify the variety of the product in the case of synthetic textiles. The plan also provides for the total wage bill of the enterprise, our profits, funding, and outlays for futher capital construction. The enterprise Party Committee is elected every two years by the Party members of the enterprise. There is also an enterprise Management Committee headed by the enterprise director and staffed by administrators and technicians. The Workers' Committee represents workers and staff. Both the enterprise Management Committee and the Workers' Committee are led by the Party Committee.[28]

The Taiyuan Iron and Steel Company, in July 1979, conducted its enterprise planning in the same manner as the Lanzhou Chemical Industries Corporation. So does the Beijing Number 2 Textile Factory, which the author visited in 1982. In industries in which there are provincial and local departments involved as intermediary organizations in planning, the process differs only in the layers of hierarchy required to approve or modify a plan. For instance, at the Jiuquan Handicrafts Factory, which produces cups and figurines for export as well as for sale in major Chinese cities, the plan provided by the Ministry of Foreign Trade may not be modified, but additional production requirements may be levied by provincial or local planners.

Under the existing planning system the factory directors and worker-managers operate under the general influence of Party committees. This parallels the phenomenon documented by Xue Muqiao at the state level, where the "government has been replaced by the Party in economic management."[29] The planning process has not changed significantly since 1975, when Rawski received a briefing on economic planning at the Capital Iron and Steel Company in Beijing.[30] Trapped in a paradox, the Party is unable to respond to these problems with clear programs. On the one hand, the Party says that "workers should have the final say in a socialist enterprise," while at the same time it affirms that "the Chinese Communist Party, as the core of leadership for the Chinese people, is of course the force directing a socialist enterprise."[31]

Given the institutional barriers built into Chinese planning by the Party ideology and the geographical constraints that require centralized planning, it seems unlikely that the Party will significantly modify its economic planning policies. Indeed, the solution to the problems may undermine the very authority of the Party and be tantamount to relinquishing claims to being "the core of leadership." Instead, the Party ensures political control of the planning process by exercising its authority through Communist Party members on the workers' and management committees responsive to central guidance. Consider the composition of planning committees at the enterprises in table 2, which illustrates the extent of Party influence in the committees. At the Inner Mongolia #2 Wool Factory and Yu Menkou Commune, the enterprise management committees were composed of the same people as the Party committee. The Party secretaries were the enterprise managers. Although there were large workers' committees, only two members of

Table 2
Party Influence in Management

Place	Party Committee Size	Management Comm. Members on Party Committee	Workers Committee Members on Party Committee
Inner Mongolia #2 Wool Factory Hohhot (1979)	7	5 (Total management 17)	2 (Total committee 15)
Yun Menkou People's Commune Chengdu, (1982)	13	12 (Total management 19	2 (Total committee 21)
Yan Tan People's Commune, Lanzhou (1983)	17	13 (Total management 21	2 (Total committee 19)

the workers' committee were on the Party committee. Consequently, because the Party insists that its own committee must guide the enterprise, workers have a negligible amount of influence on factory operation.

Such a relationship is objectionable only if Party domination of the workers' and management committees leads to a general lack of control for the workers of the enterprises they legally own. The review of contemporary Chinese literature in chapter 4 reflects a general dissatisfaction among workers over cadre privilege and the lack of self-determination in the enterprise. During the Socialist Democracy Movement, discussed next, more open complaints about the system of ownership in China surfaced.

ECONOMIC OWNERSHIP AND THE SOCIALIST DEMOCRACY MOVEMENT

In an open letter to the president of the United States published in a Chinese dissident journal on the occasion of U.S. recognition of the PRC, one Chinese author said,

> There exist in our status quo despotic dictatorship, bureaucracy, carrying on official business for private gain, persecution of the masses, the blossoming

of only one flower and only one school of thought speaking out [the Party]. People have no freedom to select employment, change residence, or publish their own opinions or works. Citizens dare not to criticize leaders and their own government, dare not run counter to the "opinions of their superior officers," and so forth.[32]

The entire system of appointing cadre and managers in enterprises was the object of condemnation by the Socialist Democracy Movement. One Chinese dissident, Lu Min, compared the system of conferring cadre ranks in enterprise to a class system without individual ownership, almost paraphrasing the definition of economic ownership presented in the previous section. That is, the form of authority exercised by cadre makes these cadre owners of the means of production.[33] The problem, according to Lu Min, was that "persons at all levels are appointed by their respective upper levels and are not elected by the people."[34]

The source of this dissent was not simply the matter of the manner in which cadre were appointed; a second major issue was the lack of meaningful authority vested in the elected leading groups of various workshops. In the second issue of *Beijing zhiqun* [*Beijing Spring*], Lu Min called for the elimination of all power belonging to basic-level Party administrators and organizations. Lu charged that the basic-level Party organizations undermined workers' authority: "Although the leaders of shifts and groups, sections and workshops are elected by the workers in a democratic way, they cannot do much because the Party organizations in basic-level units have the final say in crucial matters and matters of concern to workers. These elected section and workshop leaders do not have much actual power."[35]

Lu thought that the solution to these problems lay in bestowing authority on the populace to supervise the Communist Party, which ruled in its name. The proletariat, in Lu's proposal, was to be permitted to supervise Party members and to "dismiss those Party cadres who go against the interests of the people."[36] Otherwise, he implied, a new class composed of bureaucrats and career Party cadre would emerge, "turning public ownership into private ownership."[37]

Wei Jingsheng, a former People's Liberation Army (PLA) officer, published attacks on the Party that challenged the CCP to provide basic rights of self-determination to the citizens. Wei's name became synonymous with the struggle by Chinese workers for producers' rights under socialism. He reminded the workers that in the eyes of the Party "service to the society is limitless"; therefore "the dictatorship of the proletariat is a variation of Russian autocracy—Chinese socialist autocracy."[38] Genuine socialist ownership and self-determination, according to Wei, meant a total transfer of political-economic power to the workers:

> What is true democracy? It means the right of the people to choose their own representatives to work according to their will and in their interests. Only this can be called true democracy. Furthermore, the people must have the authority to replace representatives at any time. Thus, the representatives can not continue to deceive others in the name of the people.[39]

Wei drew a parallel between the Soviet Union and China, claiming that the development of the economy was a tool for the benefit of a "privileged few." The country's producers, according to Wei, received only the "leftovers of the privileged."[40]

Self-determination was not the only issue on which the dissidents focused. The rule of a single party, under a single ideology, was another source of their ire. Dissidents sought a pluralistic approach to government within the Marxian framework. One unidentified author suggested that the rebellious thought of the dissidents was a product of their daily experience under dictatorial control by Mao Zedong, then the Gang of Four: "If the existence and triumph of Marxism-Leninism and Mao Zedong thought must rely on the bloody suppression of all opposing views, we as clear-minded youths of the 20th century are not prepared to tolerate it."[41] The regime of Deng Xiaoping was seen as simply another dictatorship that attacked loyal Chinese citizens by labeling them anarchists and "class enemies."

It was not only in regard to urban issues that complaints about Party autocracy surfaced. The chronic problem of low agricultural productivity was tied to the lack of democracy and self-determination in the countryside.[42] The improved production levels from the contract guarantee system illustrate that this may, indeed, be true. The Party was enjoined to expand its understanding of democracy to include not only political democracy but also economic and production democracy:

> Chairman Mao led us in the construction of a new China and of a socialist society which brought liberation for workers and peasants, and also political

liberation. However, in many systems and organizations in our national economy bureaucratism has grown rapidly, hampering the speedy development of production and preventing the masses from controlling production. In many economic units production is under the control of a small group of men, orders had to be carried out exactly as given, work had to be performed according to the will of the superior and not according to economic laws. The lack of democracy in economic management leads to a lack of democracy in politics. If we want a system of people's democracy in politics we must insist on a system of people's democracy in economic management.[43]

What was the basis for the dissidents' protests? How widespread was the abuse of privilege by cadre? Ye Wenfu, in the poem "General, You Must Not Do This," accused cadre at the highest levels of CCP officialdom of deep corruption.[44] His poem allegedly told the story of a senior general of the PLA who, after rehabilitation following Mao's death, was reinstated to an important leadership position. According to the poem, the general dismantled a nursery school and built a villa for his own use costing "several hundred thousand" *yuan*. The poem charges that the general had lost his revolutionary spirit. It indicts the senior ranks of the army and Party, implying that they had built houses and gardens—that they had no concerns other than their own selfish interests and the interests of their families.

In the poem "It's Fine," published in the dissident journal *Beijing zhiqun*, an anonymous author charged that virtually all officialdom is concerned primarily with the maintenance of special privilege.[45] Notwithstanding arguments in defense of the generals,[46] "It's Fine" sums up popular feeling among the socialist democrats and their complaints about the behavior of senior Party officials in this verse: "Officials know that democracy is good, to have special privileges, one must not forget that."[47] In a manner reminiscent of Liu Binyan's story "Between Human and Demon," the accusation that the Party had turned into an instrument for the maintenance of special privilege for a few select cadre reappears.

Poetry and literature do not provide empirical evidence of corruption and malfeasance of office. Evidence of this sort often must be gleaned from veiled press references or rumors in Hong Kong periodicals, or from reports by Western correspondents in China. However, the CCP, in a campaign that followed the suppression of the Socialist Democracy Movement, seemed to respond to the charges against cadre.

This response is a tacit admission that the charges by Chinese dissidents were true: cadre malfeasance was widespread.

In what appears to be an attempt to avoid a large-scale mass movement that questioned CCP legitimacy in the manner of Poland's Solidarity movement, Deng Xiaoping initiated a rectification campaign and purge of Party members patterned on the 1942–1944 Yanan rectification.[48] This campaign to establish a "socialist spiritual civilization" (*shehui zhuyi jingshen wenming*) confirmed the charges by members of the Socialist Democracy Movement and provided a unique opportunity to explore incidents of cadre corruption. The Party Central Discipline Inspection Commission documented the way cadre function as "economic owners" of the means of production.

THE "NEW CLASS" OR CRIMINAL ACTIVITY?

Between December 1981 and December 1982 there were 160 separate references in major Chinese newspapers to incidents of malfeasance of office by Party and state cadre (see table 3). This does not mean that there were only 160 incidents—the committee reported 192,000 incidents—it means only that judicious research can document that many reports. In one case as many as nine of the eleven members of a county CCP standing committee were involved in bribery and embezzlement.[49] In another case 95 state cadres, 78 of whom were members of the Communist Party, were involved in a ring that sold automobiles illegally.[50] Each report involves more than one cadre and sometimes a whole network of them.

One source of information on the rectification campaign was the national newspaper *Renmin ribao*. However, that periodical provides news coverage of interest primarily to Beijing and information of national scope. In order to obtain information from provincial and local newspapers, as well as to have access to transcripts of domestic Chinese radio broadcasts, this study utilizes the daily reports published by the U.S. government's Foreign Broadcast Information Service (FBIS). The FBIS translations, although they do not provide blanket coverage of all news in China, devote sections to regional newspapers and radio broadcasts. Therefore the translations are an invaluable research tool if one does not have access to all of China's newspapers.

There were reports of abuses of privilege by state and Party cadre from all but five of the 29 provinces, autonomous regions, and munic-

Table 3
Reports of Cadre Malfeasance

Province	Seizure of land or housing from peasants	Privileges, bureaucratic behavior, poor work style	Speculation, bribery, embezzeling, smuggling	Illegal aid to relatives for school, houses, job, etc.	Total
Anhui	-	1	2	-	3
Beijing Shi	2	2	9	2	15
Fujian	1	1	1	1	4
Gansu	-	2	3	-	5
Guangdong	4	3	7	3	17
Guangxi	-	-	1	-	1
Guizhou	-	-	1	-	1
Hebei	2	2	2	2	8
Heilongjiang	-	1	1	1	3
Henan	-	-	-	-	-
Hubei	-	-	-	-	-
Hunan	-	1	1	-	2
Jiangsu	-	2	2	2	6
Jiangxi	1	1	1	1	4
Jilin	-	1	-	-	1
Liaoning	2	2	2	2	8
Nei Monggol	1	-	1	-	2
Ningxia	-	-	-	-	-
Qinghai	-	-	-	-	-
Shaanxi	1	-	-	-	1
Shandong*	-	-	1	-	1
Shanghai Shi	-	1	1	-	2
Shanxi*	4	-	1	2	7
Sichuan	1	1	3	1	6
Tianjin Shi	1	1	1	-	3
Xinjiang	-	-	-	1	1
Xizang	-	-	-	-	-
Yunnan	1	-	4	2	7
Zhejiang	-	1	3	-	4
Undesig. Loc.*	7	17	20	4	48
Total	·28	30	68	24	160

SOURCE: RMRB; Foreign Broadcast Information Service (FBIS)—Daily Reports, China (December 1, 1981 through November 30, 1982).

*One report of the sale of a woman and rape.

ipalities with provincial status in China. No cases were reported in the press in the minority provinces of Xizang, Ningxia, and Qinghai. Perhaps because the central government is already wrestling with problems in cadre-minority relations, reports of cadre malfeasance in these provinces were suppressed. The other two provinces that had no reported occurrences of cadre abuse of office were Henan and Hubei. There is no explanation for the dearth of information on these last two provinces. Their governors are not so well connected to the central leadership or influential that one would expect them to have been spared embarrassment. It is likely that similar abuses occurred throughout China.

Generally, the reports concerning cadre malfeasance are geographically distributed in the manner one would expect: central market areas where there is major foreign and domestic commercial activity, financial centers, and the capitol were the locales of the most numerous reports. Almost 20 percent of the incidents were reported without reference to the site of the incident.

The majority of incidents reported (68) concerned Party cadres involved in financial speculation for personal profit, bribery, embezzlement, and smuggling. The second most numerous category of incidents (40) concerned cadre who sought special privileges (e.g., personal servants, trips abroad) because of their position, engaged in bureaucratic behavior (a category the Chinese use to refer to a person who ignores responsibilities and makes no decisions), and discharged their duties with a "poor work style." Although the latter term is not fully defined, references to "poor work style" are often accompanied by references to the pamphlet "On the Basic Guiding Principles for Inner Party Political Life" and references to Liu Shaoqi's lecture "How to Be a Good Communist," which call for cadre to *selflessly* "serve the people."[51] A third category of incidents reported in the press involved 28 cases of Party cadre who had used their position to seize land or occupy housing that either belonged or was allocated to peasants.[52] The final major category of incidents concerned 24 cases in which cadre had used their positions to provide unlawful help to family members to obtain entrance to schools, obtain housing, find employment, or avoid prosecution for crimes. As the reader reviews representative cases presented herein, it may be worthwhile to refer back to the accusations about such behavior in contemporary literature.

In Zhejiang Province, at the Xinsheng Commune in Yongjia County, Party cadre organized and supervised a ring of 23 households that requisitioned state materials and then manufactured kitchen knives for private sale. The same ring, in conjunction with others in Wencheng County, compiled primary and middle school reference materials and, using state property, published and marketed these materials at a profit of 1.1 million *yuan* (U.S. $1 = .64 *yuan*). The cadre ringleader of this group made a profit of 17,000 *yuan*.[53] The primary legal issue in this case was not that the commune used its initiative to produce commodities for which there was a demand; such initiative is acceptable today in socialist China. The provincial Central Discipline Inspection Commission took the cadres to task for misappropriating state property for personal use and for using the profit from the sales for lining their own pockets—no taxes were paid on the income. Prosperity is encouraged in rural enterprises, as is individual initiative, but not out of state coffers.[54]

In Guangdong Province there were reports that Ye Jianying, the elder statesman and marshal of the People's Liberation Army, as well as his staff, were involved in a smuggling ring.[55] Although speculative, these reports fanned the flames of the fire lit by Ye Wenfu, who implicated senior army officers with his poem "General, You Must Not Do This." The charges against Ye Jianying, however, were never substantiated.

As the reporting of cadre malfeasance increased, the Party responded with enjoinders in its official organ *Hongqi* (*Red Flag*) cautioning cadre against such behavior:

> Unhealthy trends, for instance bureaucracy, seeking personal privilege, pursuing private interests, and so on are expressions of the old society's ideologies which serve the exploiting system. However, there are still some elements left over from the past which continue to exert an influence. This is because the socialist system is new, with a short history. After the Party seized power a change occurred in the thinking of certain elements. They forgot or even threw away the Party's fine tradition and work style. They adored and emulated the bad habits of the old society. Because of the evil practices and influences of the Lin Biao and Jiang Qing cliques remnants of feudalism, bourgeois thinking, anarchism, and unbridled egoism were on the upsurge. . . . These vestiges of the old society will eventually be overcome by the highly developed material and spiritual civilizations which can be established in our country.[56]

In analyzing these cases the Party equated dishonesty with capitalism, dividing "one into two" and concluding that any cadre guilty of such behavior had joined the ranks of "the enemy." The question of whether such activities were a result of human weakness or were a by-product of access to the control of the means of production apparently was never entertained by Party ideologists. Instead, human weaknesses were categorized as having a class nature and attributed to capitalist influence.

Jin Wenbing, the deputy secretary of the CCP Committee of Hejin County, Taiyuan Province, took advantage of his authority to allocate housing and land and built private houses for himself, his sons, and his daughters.[57] In addition, Jin rented out unused houses under his supervision to other persons, becoming a "cadre landlord." All of the profits from these illegal rentals were kept for his personal use.[58] Similar incidents occurred in Fujian Province, where Party cadre built private homes with the labor of individuals under their supervision and subsequently sold the houses for their own profit.[59] In these cases the cadre involved a whole network of other officials in their illicit activities.

These problems were apparently widespread enough that *Hongqi* began to hint that the children of cadre began to take on the characteristics of a new class, stating that cadre children "regard themselves a special people, separated by dress, eating habits, work place, and education."[60] In one incident that appeared in a Hong Kong newspaper, the grandson of Chu De, the revolutionary war hero and marshal of the PLA, was reportedly arrested for "irregular economic activities which insured his personal comfort."[61] In addition, because of his grandfather's status, the young man had allegedly obtained private house guards from the military.

The Hong Kong press also rumored that in Jiangsu Province the children of three senior Party cadre—Premier Zhao Ziyang, Politburo member and Shanghai Mayor Peng Chong, and PLA General Zhang Caiqian—were arrested for a series of crimes.[62] As a result of these arrests the fathers were said to have made a self-criticism in front of their respective Party branches.

The children of senior cadre also have been routinely sent out of the country for a higher education. The children of such senior officials as Deng Xiaoping and Zhang Aiping attended U.S. universities. The son of one PLA general and Politburo member was accused of promiscuity and gambling while in Atlantic City, New Jersey and was recalled to China.[63]

In Chengdu, Sichuan Province, He Deming, son of the deputy commander of the PLA Engineering Corps unit assigned in the city, was involved in multiple rapes of women.[64] He Deming threatened the victims with persecution through his father's Party and military connections if they did not submit to his sexual advances. His accomplice in these crimes was a city policeman.

The Party admitted that some leading cadres committed acts that violated the public trust of their office; but the dishonesty was attributed to the cadres having been overcome by "sugar coated bourgeois bullets."[65] This metaphorical reference to a continuing war between capitalism and communism implied that corrupting influences came either from abroad or from influences left over from the republican period before the Communist Revolution. At no time was the suggestion entertained, as it was during the Cultural Revolution, that the corrupting influence was the very structure of power in China.

Even border areas, where a well-defined military threat to China existed, were not excluded from corruption. One county deputy secretary in Yunnan Province, bordering Vietnam, was charged with the appropriation and private sale of military ammunition.[66] In the South Sea Fleet, which is responsible for waters contiguous with Vietnam, two cadre of the PLA Logistics Department—Ji Ruichen and Chen Weizhi—accepted bribes to sell jet fuel to local enterprises.[67] Proceeds from the sales were retained by the cadres.

In Guangzhou, the secretary of the Guangzhou Municipal CCP Committee, who concurrently served as chief of the Guangzhou Telecommunications Bureau, was sentenced to two years in prison for corrupt activities.[68] The bureau chief, Wang Weijing, had sold for personal profit two color televisions, 98 calculators, and five watches, all procured with state funds.

The normal system of bonuses in industry was also abused; cadres paid high bonuses to themselves and accepted furniture and other goods as "bonuses in kind."[69]

The illegalities were so widespread that one article in *People's Daily* estimated that 12,000 houses had been illegally constructed and sold by cadre.[70] However, when the Party finally acted against these cadre, only 469 rooms in 169 of the illegally constructed houses were confiscated. At the time that the rectification campaign to correct the abuses took hold in Liaoning Province, the newspaper *Shenyang Daily* summed up the criminal acts this way: "Some cadres have illegally arranged jobs for children, relatives and friends, occupied more housing than they need, embezzled public funds and property, built private houses on public land, established illicit connections to have their children enrolled at schools, and illegally purchased rationed goods.''[71]

A similar commentary from the *Jinan Daily* underscored the seriousness of the legitimation crisis faced by the Party:

> Although some Communist party members talk about fighting for communism all their lives, what they actually seek are comfortable and easy lives, positions (the higher the better), money (the more the better), dwellings (the bigger the better—some even plan to build villas) and children, (anything possible to seek practical gains for them). They pursue evil practices, such as getting back-door benefits, establishing personal relations, robbing for selfish ends, acting in public service for private ends, taking advantage of the masses, collectives and the state by utilizing overt and covert means and so on. It is obvious that these so-called Party members, apart from not playing the vanguard role, severely impair the Party's image and lessen its prestige.[72]

The editorial staff of *People's Daily*, in response to theoretical discussions about the conception of class in China, published a series of articles concerning the basis of class stratification in socialist society. The thrust of the discussion responded indirectly to charges by Chinese dissidents that the Communist Party formed a ''new class.'' One commentator, Wang Zhengping, denied that classes could emerge from a political party because ''relations of production and relations of the systems of ownership are the basic decisive characteristics in deciding class. Determinations of class are made according to the standards of relations of production and relations of the systems of ownership.''[73]

In an affirmation of Wang Zhengping's argument, two commentators in the Party ideological journal *Hongqi* wrote an article that responded directly to charges that the Party was developing into a new class. Lin Boye and Shen Zhe declared that it was ''scientifically impossible for a class of bureaucrats to emerge from a Communist party.''[74] Classes, according to Lin and Shen, ''are demarcated according to the relations in which they stand to production and the system of ownership.''[75] Therefore, according to the ''laws of the historical development of society and Marxist-Leninist teaching,'' these two defenders of the Party asserted, ''political parties can only be part of, or represent, a class . . . classes can not emerge from a political party.''[76]

The commentary denied that a class had developed in the CCP and decreed that even if a communist party degenerated and lost sight of its goal, it was theoretically impossible for that party to give birth to a class from within itself.

Lin and Shen further argued that older cadres, particularly those who had served through the war against Japan and the revolution, had earned a few extra privileges. Even with the extra privileges, according to the commentators, such cadres enjoy only a slightly better standard of living than the average person.[77]

Lin and Shen's arguments have some merit. There are circumstances that call for differences in opportunities and living standards, even in a society that espouses egalitarianism and collective ownership: a factory director might have great demands on his or her time, requiring executive assistants, secretaries, and convenient personal transportation. The managerial abilities of such a person may be so valuable as to render the individual less effective if time were taken in the preparation of routine correspondence or in travel on public transport. The same is true of a senior government or military official. Certain persons, because of their positions, may require representational living quarters—for instance, those who deal with foreign businessmen or diplomats.

The rational distribution of such perquisites, however, does not constitute license to abuse one's office. The rigid insistence by the CCP and its defenders on the juridical definition of ownership is a weak argument and avoids a response to the issue of whether legal ownership corresponds to control of the means of production. The average person in China, without the authority of an official position backed by the proper political pedigree (CCP membership), is simply not in a position to administer, misappropriate, or otherwise dispose of large amounts of publicly owned property. The only access to such power is through official position, and the ultimate authority to set policy directing the allocation of public resources is derived from Party membership. For this reason, the concept of economic ownership is crucial to understanding political economy in China.

A case in Gansu Province provides an example of this. A prefectual commercial bureau director, who was concurrently the bureau Communist Party secretary, supplied ration certificates and letters of authorization for purchases to a peasant who was a local commune member.[78] The peasant then used the certificates to purchase 44 sewing machines and 47 bicycles from state-owned commercial stores. After keeping two bicycles and one sewing machine for his personal use, the peasant sold the others for over 7,930 *yuan*, which he split with the Party official.[79]

Profiteering of this sort is not possible without the cooperation of a Party member. The only people who have access to commodity allocation, housing allocation, and the allocation of employment are officials and cadre. Even if an official is not a member of the CCP, authority over and supervision of the official is exercised by the Party. Policy is set by the Party. Oversight is a Party responsibility. The senior officials of the country are Communist Party members.

In China the economic owners of the means of production are the members of the Party committee of an enterprise. They may be assisted by technocrats and intellectuals, they may operate with the cooperation of workers' committees, but it is the Party committee that exercises functional control over the means of production.

The CCP associates criminal acts such as smuggling, profiteering, speculation, swindling, and bribery with capitalism. All forms of corruption, moral or financial, are treated as bourgeois conduct that reflects a continuing struggle between the capitalist and the communist line in a socialist society.[80] Thus the problem of cadre malfeasance has been translated by the CCP into a question of class. By doing so, the Party avoids the charges that its domination of society may have produced a new class of owners.

The issue of criminal activity, however, is not one of capitalism versus communism. Immoral or criminal activity—indeed, the very conception of morality in the separation of the public and private realms or property and responsibility—has no class nature. These are questions of personal integrity and human frailty. Violation of the public trust and the use of a public position for personal gain are illegal in any social collectivity.

There is an existential tension between the self and the collectivity in any society, not just in socialist society. The moral prohibitions against violations of the public trust are as strong in capitalist states as they are in socialist states. Such morality is implicit in the very concept of public office. If one were to make a table to correlate the incidence of official corruption in the United States, it would likely be longer than the table produced from the Chinese newspapers. Consider, for instance, the number of senior officials in the Reagan administration that have violated or may have abused the trust of their public office—over 50.[81] These cases include the allegations of improper lobbying by Michael Deaver, the petty cash indiscretions of National Security Adviser Richard V. Allen, mortgage loans at favorable rates to presidential staffer Joseph W. Canzeri, and questions about stock and securities trading to the tune of between $1.9 and $4.5 million by Director of Central Intelligence William J. Casey.[82]

The critical issue is not that corruption exists (although the level of corruption in a society is certainly a mark of the strength or weakness of its moral and ethical institutions), but whether authority, the right to public office, and control of political and economic institutions should flow from a single source that legitimizes itself.

The CCP argues in its theoretical journals that it is impossible for a class of bureaucrats to appear in a socialist society because bureaucrats are a stratum of the class holding power.[83] The Party journal denies that politics and ideology may be used as standards for class demarcation; it rejects standards from Western sociologists that take "income, profession, cultural standards, and ideology" as determinants of class demarcation.[84] According to the journal *Hongqi*, "classes are only demarcated according to the relations in which they stand to production and the system of ownership."[85]

Despite the Party's denials, inquiries by the Central Discipline Investigation Commission support the argument that income, adherence to a dominant ideology, and placement in the Party (or state) bureaucracy are significant factors in class demarcation and social stratification in China. The orthodox and unrevised Marxian conception of class is not a viable way to understand social stratification or political and economic power in China. The concepts must be altered to account for managers whose control of production and allocation amounts to functional ownership.

The concluding chapter attempts an analysis of Chinese society that stratifies the population according to its relationship to the means of production but considers their relationship to the centralized power of the state and Party. This relationship affects income, living standards, and economic ownership. The discussion considers the relationship between a citizen and the control system for enterprise and state economic planning as important factors in political economy stratifying a populace under socialism.

6

Class and Stratification in China Today

In China, because of the structure of the state planning system, one cannot directly correlate class categories based on the ownership of the means of production with the awareness and articulation of political interest as Marx did, for instance, in nineteenth-century England. Economic management in China, as in other planned socialist economies, is designed to balance production and consumption (supply and demand) among the sectors of the economy (e.g., agriculture, light industry, heavy industry, transport).[1]

As a result, because the legal owner in a socialist state has limited control over the means of production, political interest is only partially articulated in terms of the nature of a worker's relationship to the means of production. Aggregate political interests come to have a more fundamental focus: on improving the relative emphasis placed on a given sector of the economy by the central planning process, on increasing the autonomy allowed the local Communist Party committee in influencing the enterprise decision-making process, and on securing more political power vis-à-vis the Communist Party (expressed in terms of worker self-determination by members of China's dissident movement).

The concept of class to a great extent has lost its currency among the populace as a means to identify political interest in the socialist state. After the abuses committed during the Cultural Revolution in the name of class struggle, the very concept of class, for many Chinese people, has come to signify the pursuit of factional Party interests. Class analysis by the Party consistently refers back to a "line" struggle against "enemies" who represent the "capitalist line." The reason for this phenomenon is the epistemology involved. Instead of engaging in politico-economic analysis, different factions of the Party have dichotomized society to serve their own interests or to advance their ideological line.

All of this should not be construed to say that class analysis is of no utility in China (or in any other socialist state). Using the criteria for the separation of classes established by Marx and Lenin, there are identifiable social classes in China and different relations to the means of production.[2] However, the reader should understand that an analysis of class is like a snapshot: it shows a web of relations at a given moment or a given stage of development. As technology and economic conditions develop and change, as the foreign trade and foreign economic relations of China change, so do class relations. One may demonstrate different aspects of social relations depending on the perspective used: the shared ownership of the means of production, the distribution of income and housing, or the authority to undertake substantive political or economic decisions. But the very use of one perspective may hide attributes that might be visible were another perspective adopted. In classical Marxist analysis the most salient factor dividing classes has been private ownership. In the socialist state class analysis must illuminate other factors that are more significant determinants of sociopolitical and socioeconomic status. The question of income distribution is still important, for it affects life-style; more important are political and ethical questions about who has the right to make decisions. The most important question in analyzing classes and political interest in socialist states hinges on the Marxian concept of alienation.

A primary tenet of Marxist ideology is that there should be a politico-economic relationship that allows members of the body politic, as the legal owners of the means of production, to make social, political, and economic decisions about socially owned property and the governance of the state.[3] Any departure from this condition of self-determination was judged by Marxists to be tantamount to the estrangement of humanity from itself and from the products of its labor.[4] The purpose of Marx's critique of capitalist political economy was to return human society—which, for Marx, was reduced to human engagement in the social production of material life—to a reconciliation with its own labor and with nature in order to transcend the state of alienation in which Marx believed humans lived.[5] Marx believed that the "whole produce of labor belongs to the workers"; his goal was to empower the worker to control the fruits of that labor.[6]

ALIENATION: ECONOMIC, POLITICAL, AND SOCIAL

In Marx's interpretation, human labor in the service of a capitalist was reified human self-alienation.[7] The fact that workers could be hired and fired, bought and sold like commodities was for him half of an equation that amounted to the surrender of humanity for the worker. The second half of that equation was the surrender of the products of human labor:

> This fact [that workers become commodities without control over the products of their labor] simply means that the object that labor produces, its product, stands opposed to it as something alien, as a power independent of the producer. The product of labor is labor embodied and made material in an object, it is the objectification of labor. The realization of labor is its objectification. In the sphere of political economy this objectification appears as a loss of reality for the worker, as a loss of and bondage to the object, and appropriation as estrangement, as alienation.[8]
>
> It [communist society] is the complete restoration of man to himself as a social, i.e., human being, a restoration which has become conscious. . . . It is the genuine resolution of the conflict between man and nature, between man and man, and the true resolution between existence and being, between objectification and self-affirmation, between freedom and necessity, between individual and species. It is the solution of the riddle of history and knows itself to be the solution.[9]

Thus the success or failure of a form of social organization, by the application of Marx's principles as stated above, ought to be measured by the level of integration between the laborer and the product. Self-determination (or self-management) becomes the goal of the political system. This integration is most often identified, in China as well as in Eastern Europe, with the authority for the worker to allocate work and to plan the economy.[10]

In practice, however, certain factors—political, social, and economic—have resisted the restoration of community to human life.[11] In the economic sphere the primary factor has been the division of labor as an economy of effort, which has fragmented the process of production. Marx and Engels associate the division of labor with the establishment of the initial estrangement between "the separate individual or the individual family and the communal interest of all individuals who have intercourse with one another."[12] They relate this estrangement, or alienation, to the basis of the contradiction of interests between the individual and the collectivity (represented by the state); a contradiction that extends itself into modern society and is reflected in the tensions among worker, enterprise, and the state plan.[13] For China, this tension is recognized by economists from the Party and central government, but the tension seems to defy resolution. Xue Muqiao writes that "if unified state leadership over the economy is interpreted as centralized management and is allowed to weaken the power of the local authorities and enterprises to manage their own affairs, our economic life will stagnate." He goes on to say that "on the other hand, over-emphasis on independent management by the local authorities and enterprises and a weakening of unified state leadership over the economy would lead to anarchy."[14]

This tension would likely be healthy if it was mediated by a dialogue between worker and state. Instead, critics of the Communist Party in China complain that centralized management is so pervasive that "production is controlled by a small group of men."[15] One consequence of this rigid control is that it forces workers to confront their own subordination to the Party and the state plan sponsored by the Party. Discourse is eliminated by Party authority, and the dissident laborer or intellectual is subjected to objurgation by the Party; citizens become alienated economically from what they produce and where they work.

As the previous chapter discussed, one economic factor that has fragmented the process of production and the management system in China is the uneven distribution of resources. The redistribution of these resources to support production, which is complicated by transportation bottlenecks, has been a major impediment to improving planning, production, and management in China. The transport infrastructure in China is inadequate to distribute the resources available as they are needed to support balanced production and economic development.[16] More seriously, officials often use their influence to bypass the planned use of transportation assets.

In the social sphere the existence of biological differences in intelligence and natural abilities—which often creates a hierarchy of tasks in social relations of production—has proved a major impediment to the restoration of a sense of human community. People simply have different capacities to learn and to work. They have different interests, and these differences are reflected in the question of whether or not the Party needs to address the question of "bourgeois right." Should superior contribution (to the state or to production) be rewarded in a manner commensurate with the amount of work or the quality of work contributed? (This is the form of reward under bourgeois right.) Or should the distribution of goods be commensurate with need, as is suggested in *The Communist Manifesto*?

Finally, in the political sphere the need for some form of central direction and management in the state produces an elite. This elite, whether it is called a stratum of the working class or a "new class," comes to enjoy material privileges and the perquisites of position or high office. In all societies an elite has a tendency to alienate itself politically from its constituency by virtue of its living a different lifestyle. In the Marxist one-party state, according to critics such as Mihailo Markovic, the elite becomes a self-perpetuating bureaucratic institution.[17] Its position and political authority are never challenged by alternative political forces in the country (such as the Socialist Democracy Movement). Even if there are challenges (as there have been in China, Hungary, Czechoslovakia, and Poland), the Party's authority is constitutionally guaranteed by (1) the requirements for the maintenance of a "people's democratic dictatorship"; (2) the Party's control over forces of repression (police and army); and (3) the Party's ability, as "the vanguard of the working class," to discount the opinions of opponents by labeling them products of "false consciousness."[18]

Once this elite of managers is developed and comes to enjoy privilege, it may cling permanently to its political and material privileges, refusing to shift power back to the legal owners of the means of production—the workers. On the other hand, the elite could "find within itself the moral strength and consistency" voluntarily to set itself aside as a power elite and allow increasing self-management of the economy.[19] Unfortunately, this has not been the practice in Marxist-Leninist states. Once communist parties have gained control of the state, they have ruthlessly eliminated challeges to their right to rule.

Signs of Alienation

The portrayal of China's power elite in that nation's contemporary literature reveals a perception among its authors that there is a general lack of "strong moral resolve" on the part of the Communist Party to set itself aside. The discussion of the Party's domination of both enterprise management and state planning in the last chapter underscores the manner in which trends toward self-management are severely circumscribed by institutional as well as geographical constraints in China. The economic ownership of the means of production by the Party bureaucracy, coupled with Party domination of both the social relations of production and political life in China, increasingly alienates the Chinese people from the Chinese Communist Party, creating a legitimation crisis for the CCP.

At the same time, there are trappings that symbolize for the people that a revolution has taken place, that they have been given new privileges. Places such as the Ming Tombs, the Sun Yat-sen Mausoleum, the Summer Palace, the Temple of Heaven, and the old Imperial City, once closed to all but the emperors and ruling elite, are now open to the public. Any Chinese citizen may visit the Great Hall of the People. But there is little mention of the "New Forbidden City," which is what Zhongnanhai has become. Here, surrounded by an "imperial" guard, members of the Party center never receive outsiders. This compound, situated west of the old imperial Forbidden City, stands surrounded by walls and guards—impenetrable except for the very senior ranks of Party and government. Cadre of the highest levels are said to live inside Zhongnanhai in relative splendor with servants, automobiles, and special stores at their disposal. In the same compound, it is rumored, the Gang of Four and others in disfavor were held under close arrest.

The CCP acknowledges the legitimation crisis it has created. One 1982 commentary in *Renmin ribao* discussed the inability of the Polish and Czechoslovakian Communist parties to satisfy the "social contract" in those countries.[20] Commentators noted that a reform of the Party cadre system in China was needed if the Party wanted to retain the trust of the proletariat.[21] The result of continuing political, social, and economic alienation, according to the *Renmin ribao* commentator, would be that the "proletarian political party, which is the core of the superstructure, will no longer be trusted and supported by the people." The commentary went on to say that "experiences abroad and at home have all proven this stern truth."[22]

One sign of such alienation is, of course, the very existence of loose coalitions seeking political expression, such as the Socialist Democracy Movement. Another phenomenon symptomatic of a schism between the CCP and its constituency is the way in which Party leadership is portrayed in the popular fiction in *Renmin Wenxue*. But the major manifestation of this alienation is the Party's inability to distinguish between good and evil, right and wrong. Socialist society is portrayed by the Party as a progressive force that continually improves—a progression of superlatives that, although susceptible to "mistakes" (such as the Cultural Revolution), has no inherent evil. Evil and wrongdoing exist only in "the other society," the capitalist and Western world. When instances of wrongdoing occur in socialist society, the Party charges that they are a result of outside influence or are the vestiges of capitalism in China; evil is an alien penetration.

The issue of alienation forms the basis for the rejection of Marxist class analysis by many Chinese. The Party, however, has avoided confronting the problem of alienation by arguing that a people (class) cannot be alienated by themselves. Li Yanshi, in a commentary in the *Nanfang ribao* on January 30, 1984, has argued that there must be limits to any participation by "the masses" in the decision-making process of the state. Li argues that the state must issue "compulsory orders" but that this is not "the alienation of power." He insists that the masses adhere to the principles of "democratic centralism" and "exercise their freedom to advance the socialist system."

At the same time, the Party has glossed over other significant factors used by social scientists in class analysis: life-style, access to education, income, and participation in self-management. Notwithstanding efforts to side-step the issue of alienation, a central theoretical problem with which the Party has wrestled is the relationship of intellectuals to social classes. While attempting a class analysis we must also consider this question.

MENTAL LABOR AND MANUAL LABOR

Mental laborers, or intellectuals, are not direct producers of anything. Defining the role of intellectual in capitalist as well as socialist society has been problematic for Marxists.[23] There is a difference between mental labor and physical labor that is a function of the division of labor, a difference that obviously manifests itself in work that is physically easier for mental laborers. Intellectuals, therefore, are generally said to belong to the class that they support. That is, according to Marxist theory, they attach themselves to a class through their skills or through the means by which they can earn their incomes. Ironically, intellectuals have been regarded not as a class but as commodities to be bought or sold as needed. Lenin said of them:

> We are still in need of technicians, agronomists, chemists, architects, etc., it is true, but if the worst comes to the worst we can always buy them just as well as the capitalists buy them, and if a severe example is made of a few of the traitors among them—for traitors there are sure to be—they will find it to their own advantage to deal fairly with us. But apart from these specialists, among whom I also include schoolteachers, we can get along perfectly well without the other "intellectuals." The present influx of literati and students into the party, for example, may be quite damaging if these gentlemen are not properly kept in check.[24]

On the other hand, intellectuals are recognized as the very basis of revolutionary action. For intellectuals are, after all, the founders of the Communist Party. Marx and Engels were intellectuals, Mao Zedong was an intellectual-turned-revolutionary. According to Lenin:

> The history of all countries shows that the working class, exclusively by its own effort, is able to develop only the trade-union consciousness, i.e., the conviction that it is necessary to combine in unions, fight the employers, and strive to compel the government to pass necessary labor legislation, etc. The theory of socialism, however, grew out of the philosophic, historical, and economic theories elaborated by educated representatives of the propertied classes, by intellectuals.[25]

At the present time the CCP seems to find the question of the intellectual less problematic. Intellectuals are not now regarded as a separate class. The labor of intellectuals is now treated as a form of work to be combined with manual labor in the production of a commodity.[26] According to the Party, intellectuals are part of the working class and, along with manual workers, contribute to the development of socialism.[27] Certainly there are strong arguments to support the Party's stand. Neither intellectuals nor manual workers are able fully to articulate their material interests and translate these interests into political programs or changes in the allocative process in China. Important economic decisions concerning the direction of the national economy or the direction of an enterprise may not be undertaken without the approval of the CCP. At the national level this means that the Central Committee must approve or underwrite Party decisions. At the local level the enterprise Party committee must implement policies to do the same. Therefore both intellectuals and manual laborers are relegated to the same conditions with respect to the means of production. They are legal owners, but they are subordinated to the central authority of the Party because of its functional (economic) ownership of the means of production.

In agriculture, as tables 4 and 5 illustrate, in 1979 approximately 6.5 million intellectuals were employed as staff members, including managers, at collectively owned enterprises. The numbers of persons involved are probably not so numerous that they represent a weighty or nonproductive burden on peasants, even considering the labor-intensive agricultural techniques employed in China. They represent a very small percentage (2 percent) of the agricultural population. It is more important for us to know how many of these intellectuals are members of township or brigade Communist Party committees. Table 2, in the previous chapter, provides only limited information in this regard but enough to serve to illustrate the discussion. At the two communes where the author was able to gather these data, the Party committee was dominated by the intellectuals from the management committee.

This means that intellectuals have a disproportionate influence on the management of the agricultural or industrial enterprise. If these managers, even as members of a Party committee, are responsive to the concerns of the peasants or workers in the productive branch of the economy, the imbalance is probably not important. But few surveys allow us to measure such responsiveness. John P. Burns, in a study of rural production team cadre between 1958 and 1974, concludes that at the lowest administrative levels peasant political interests are articulated through the election of production team cadre.[28] However, at levels higher than the production team major issues are determined by the more senior bodies in the Party hierarchy.[29] Burns makes the point that "a comprehensive picture of production team elections . . . must begin from an understanding of the position of the produc-

Table 4
A Breakdown of China's Labor Force as It Relates to the Ownership of the Means of Production (Figures are in thousands of persons)

Economic Sector	1979	1981	1983
Total population	970,920*	996,220	1,024,950
Total social laborers (in national economy)**	405,810	432,800	460,040
Rural labor (of which)	305,820	322,720	344,890
-Employed in agriculture	229,340	n/a	n/a
-Staff or self employed	6,840	n/a	n/a
Labor in cities and towns (of which)	99,990	110,530	115,150
-Workers and staff in state owned enterprises	76,930***	83,720	87,710
-Workers and staff in collectively owned enterprises	22,740***	25,680	27,436
-Individual laborers (self employed)	320	1,130	****

SOURCES: All 1979 data, unless otherwise noted, are from John Philip Emerson, "The Labor Force of China," p. 240. All 1981 data are from 1982 JJNJ, pp. VIII-6, VIII-66; and BR No. 48 (November 29, 1982):18-19. 1983 data and that marked *** is from the 1984 Almanac of China's Economy (Hong Kong, Modern Cultural Co.), pp. 26, 27, 34-40, 70-71, 82-85.

*Data from 1981 JJNJ, p. VI-3.

**Age ranges for the labor force are not provided. However, I assume the ages to be between about 15 or 16 and 55 years.

***1984 Almanac of China's Economy (see above).

****I cannot explain the reduction in individual laborers despite the implementation of programs in the PRC that should have significantly increased this figure.

n/a = not available

Table 5
A Breakdown of China's Labor Force as It Relates to the Productive and Nonproductive Branches of the Economy (Figures are in thousands of persons)

Branch of the Economy	1965	1979
Productive branches		
-Commune agriculture	233,980	299,340
-Industry	17,434	44,367
-Building trades	4,765	8,903
-State farms, water convervancy, forestry, and meteorology*	4,934	8,620
-Transport, post, and telecommunications	4,167	6,725
-Urban self employed**	1,170	320
Nonproductive branches		
-Commune staffs	1,360	6,480
-Trade, food and drink, service**	7,503	12,872
-Science, technology, cultural affairs, education, and health	6,508	11,310
-Urban public utilities	440	1,109
-Finance	360	504
-Government administration and mass organizations***	2,933	4,680
-Other	584	472

SOURCE: Emerson, "The Labor Force in China," p. 240.

*Meteorology should be included in the nonproductive sector.

**By 1982 there was a vast increase in the numbers of persons employed in these areas. For example, that year 6,264 persons were employed as scientists and technicians in state-owned units and 3,143 were professional health workers. See BR No. 19 (May 9, 1983):XI. Given the current emphasis on service industries (whether collective or individual) more significant increases are likely to be reflected in any forthcoming statistics.

***This figure includes only a portion of the full-time staff of the CCP. No further breakdown is available.

tion team in the Chinese political system, and the very real power of the brigade to negate election results.''[30] Even at the lowest levels of the economic and political system, the Party blocks the articulation of peasant political interest.[31]

In industry, as one might expect, the number of persons engaged in mental rather than manual labor is higher than in agriculture. As table 6 demonstrates, state-owned industry (owned by the whole people) has

Table 6
Nonproductive Labor in Industry

	Industry	Ownership	Total workers	Managerial and clerical personnel (nonproductive)
1.	Shih Wan Ceramics Factory (Guangdong)	Urban Collective	580	30
2.	Taiyuan Iron & Steel Company (Shanxi)	State	50,000	5,000
3.	NW Cotton Textile Plant #4, Xian (Shaanxi)	State	7,139	400
4.	Suzhou Embroidery Institute (Zhejiang)	Urban Collective	239	40
5.	Suzhou Lacquer-ware & Mahogany Factory (Zhejiang)	Urban Collective	700	20-25
6.	Hangzhou Machine Tool Factory (Zhejiang)	State	1,800	200

SOURCE: Wortzel, "Incentive Mechanisms and Remuneration in China," p.969.

a much higher percentage of its labor force (5–10 percent) dedicated to mental labor than does collectively owned industry. However, one can infer even from the sketchy data available that intellectuals on Party committees are more heavily represented and occupy more authoritative positions of functional control over the means of production than do manual laborers. Clearly this is a question that deserves more attention and about which more data must be obtained. However, only a few of the thirty-odd separate enterprises the author has visited in China were willing to provide these data. Only the most tentative hypotheses can be suggested based on the very limited data contained in this study.

In the Soviet Union, where such data are more readily available from published sources, a similar trend is evident in industry. In the early 1970s at the Leningrad Machine Building Plant only about 4 percent of unskilled manual laborers were Party members, whereas 20 percent of persons in skilled mental work were Party members.[32] The representation of the Party among production organizers and managers numbered 54 percent.[33] In the Tatar Republic of the USSR in 1967, 84 percent of senior management belonged to the Communist Party, whereas only 5 percent of unskilled laborers and 10 percent of skilled laborers belonged to the Party (see table 7). The level of participation in the Party drops off significantly among manual laborers and drastically among low-skilled workers. Here, when examining social stratification, it would seem that the Weberian concept of status groups is of more value as an analytical tool than is Marxist class theory.

A more illuminating view of social stratification in China, but one that requires a revision of our understanding of the orthodox Marxist term "class," is the distribution of the labor force among branches of the economy. The separation of the national economy into branches by Chinese economic planners, with the related division of the branches

Table 7
Party Makeup and Education of Socio-Occupations in the Tatar Republic of the Soviet Union: 1967

Socio-Occupational group	Percent Party Members	Years of Education	
		Tatars	Russians
Senior management	84	10	0
Middle management	62	8.4	8.2
Senior specialist	61	13.4	12.8
Middle specialist	35	10.4	10.7
Non-manual worker	36	8.5	8.4
Machine operator	15	6.2	5.6
Skilled manual worker	10	5.3	5.3
Low-skilled manual worker	7	5.1	4.0
Unskilled labor	5	5.1	3.4

SOURCE: Murray Yanowitch, Social and Economic Inequality in the Soviet Union (New York: M.E. Sharpe, 1977), p. 49.

into productive and nonproductive categories, parallels the division between manual and mental labor. In the socialist state, given the competing political and economic interests of persons employed in the various branches of the economy, it is useful to consider the disparate interests that follow from such employment.

BRANCHES OF THE ECONOMY

A common distinction in Chinese (and Marxist) economic theory is the separation of the working populace into those engaged in productive labor and those engaged in nonproductive labor. The latter category includes service or support functions. This separation forms two major branches of the economy (productive or nonproductive) that are common functions to all sectors of the economy (see table 5).[34] The basis for the separation is related to Marx's "labor theory of value," or "law of value," which hypothesizes that the value of a commodity is determined by the amount of labor embodied in it (including labor in the plant, raw materials, and production equipment) and affects resource allocation.[35] However, the labor theory of value does not directly account for time and effort expended in management, supervision, or trade. Those who work in such areas are paid from the total income of an enterprise, adding to the wage bill, but they are direct producers of nothing.[36] As should be evident from this short discussion, the relationship between the productive and nonproductive branches of the economy is so closely related both to the labor theory of value and to distinctions between mental and manual labor that no analysis is complete without considering them.

The branches of the economy serve as planning tools that account for the costs of the administration of economic production and of government. These costs must be financed from the productive branches, but they are not useful as a basis for the understanding of orthodox Marxist class relations because neither individual ownership (in the case of small traders) nor collective or state ownership provides greater leverage over the process of state planning. Legal ownership must translate into political authority in the dealings of the state and in the management of the enterprise for the orthodox Marxist concept of class to serve as a viable measure of sociopolitical conditions. In China, however, there are no intrinsic distinctions of class between productive and nonproductive labor. That is, the form that labor takes does not make the worker a member of either one class or another; nor does the form of labor make a person a member of a "ruling class." For this reason one need not distinguish between the staff members (administrators in white-collar positions and clerical workers) and the manual laborers in Chinese enterprises.

Although there are differences in bonuses between manual and mental laborers, the wages of both are based on the same eight-grade scale (table 8). If persons are classified as educators or technicians, they have the potential to earn between two and three times as much as the worker on the eight-grade system (table 9), but this still does not constitute a difference in social class. The primary consideration when undertaking a class analysis in a socialist state as a means for understanding political phenomena is not salary—which, of course, makes for a more comfortable life-style—nor is the legal ownership of the means of production any longer a major consideration, as it is in the capitalist state, because the legal ownership of the means of production cannot be translated directly into allocative power. Even enterprise administration has lost some of its importance as a means to demarcate class membership, for the mere occupation of a managerial position cannot be translated directly into allocative authority for the manager. What criteria, then, may be used to identify classes?

One must consider as foremost (1) the relative authority of persons to make decisions about the distribution of goods and services; (2) the allocation of food and housing; (3) access to educational opportunities; and (4) the structure of the labor force at an enterprise. These variables are more important than the division of labor or the legal form of ownership of the means of production to make a meaningful analysis of the social stratification in an enterprise. Such decisions about allocation, or at minimum the authority to set policy regarding the decisions and the right to supervise such decisions, are the prerogative of the CCP and its local committees. These local decisions are supervised by provincial, regional, and national Party committees. Only those who are on a Party committee may be said to have allocative power and functional control over the society. Therefore Party membership is significant when considering functional control of the means of production. Indeed, more important than mere CCP membership is service in a responsible position in the Party. Otherwise entry into the ranks of the elite cannot be translated into allocative power. Party membership is a necessary condition to achieve allocative authority.

Table 8
Salaries and Bonuses for Enterprise Production and Service Workers: 1959–1983 (Figures are in Ren Min Bi)

Salaries for Workers and Staff in Industry

Industry	Year	Grade 1	2	3	4	5	6	7	8
Anshan Iron & Co.	1959	34.5	40.7	48.1	56.8	67.1	79.3	94.0	110.4
Anshan Rough Rolling Mill	1972	3.45	40.0	48.1	56.8	67.1	79.3	84.5	110.0
Shih Wan Pottery Factory	1973	35.0	41.0	47.0	56.0	63.0	na	na	108.0
	1979	40.0	44.1	50.1	na	70.0	na	na	110.0
Hangzhou Machine Tool Factory	1979	36.0	43.0	50.2	57.2	72.0	82.3	94.1	115.0
Harbin No. 1 Dept. Store	1981	33.0	36.0	41.5	47.5	54.0	61.0	70.0	na
Lanzhou Petro-Chemicals Plant	1983	36.0	41.0	na	56.0	64.0	na	95.0	114.0

SOURCE for 1959, 1972, and 1973 figures: Charles Riskin, Workers Incentives in Chinese Industry," in China: A Reassessment of the Economy, U.S. Congress, Joint Economic Committee Print (Washington, D.C.: GPO, 1975), pp. 99, 224; source for 1981 data: Travel notes--Donald R. Cake (April 14, 1981); the 1979 and 1983 data are from my own trip notes.

Monthly Industrial Bonuses in 1979 (Non-Piecework)

Grade	Workers	Administrators/Technicians
1	9	6
2	8	5
3	7	4

SOURCE: Larry M. Wortzel, "Incentive Mechanisms and Remuneration in China," Asian Survey 21 (September 1981):973. For an explanation of bonus grades see Ibid., pp. 972-74.

Table 9
Salaries for Technicians and Educators: 1979 (Figures are in Ren Min Bi)

Position	Grade	Monthly Wage
	Technicians	
Chief Engineer	2	180
Section Head	9	100
Deputy Section Head	10	83
Technical Worker	12	59
Technical Worker	13	53
	Educators	
Professor (University)	na	250-380
Deputy Professor (University)	na	130-180
Lecturer (University)	na	70-100
Asst. Lecturer (University)	na	45-65
New Graduate (University)	na	37-44
Middle School Teacher	na	35-100
Primary School Teacher	na	50-130

SOURCE: Gathered during visits with the staffs of Hangzhou Machine Tool Factory; Hangzhou Normal University; and Chinese Academy of Social Sciences Branches at Shanghai, Beijing, and Chengdu. Published previously in Wortzel, "Incentive Mechanisms and Remuneration in China," p. 968.

INCOME DISTRIBUTION

What of income distribution—how does it relate to the question of class? Here one must consider the sector of the economy in which an individual is employed. Industrial workers enjoy roughly the same salaries. The average ratio of wage spread between the highest- and lowest-paid industrial workers is about 3.2:1, not too different from the wage spread in the United States and Western Europe in 1972.[37] The wage spread for industrial workers in the Soviet Union is 1:2, although bonuses change this picture of a more egalitarian ratio.[38]

In China in 1974, workers in state industry generally enjoyed a higher monthly wage than workers in enterprises under provincial, county, or local-level management.[39] For example, addressing 1974 conditions, Prybyla states that the average maximum wage for an employee in an industry owned by the state was 107 *yuan* per month and the minimum wage was 39 *yuan* per month, whereas in an industry under county-level management the corresponding maximum and minimum wages were 77 and 30 *yuan* per month, respectively.[40] These relative differences are still in effect today.

Party membership by itself may not directly influence income for the worker or for the technocrat who is a CCP member. Party membership does not directly influence the social benefit package available to the grass-roots-level Party member. As an example, the member of a small production unit who has been a Party member and an elected shop leader in a weaving mill in Lanzhou proudly pointed out that she drew 74 *yuan* each month as a grade-six worker. However, in the long run Party members are able to advance themselves into much higher wage brackets if they concentrate on politics, leave enterprise administration, and enter the professional ranks of the Party bureaucracy (see table 10). Furthermore, with these increases in wages comes greater authority to allocate resources.

The really great schism in income relates to employment in an economic sector, not to the form of ownership of the enterprise. Referring to table 11, it is apparent that the peasants in the rural townships in production brigades, notwithstanding the few model "ten thousand *yuan* families," earn one-third the amount of money earned by the average worker in an industrial enterprise. The average annual per capita net income for peasants has improved steadily; but, as table 12 demonstrates, 80 percent of China's 800 million persons in peasant families earn only between 150 and 500 *yuan* each year.[41] Moreover, although the entire income for a worker comes from the enterprise, only about 60 percent of the income for a peasant is provided by the production unit—the rest comes from sideline production (table 13). In 1982 only about 6.7 percent of peasant families had an average annual per capita income of over 500 *yuan*.[42] Average per capita peasant income rose from 223.44 *yuan* in 1981 to 270.11 *yuan* in 1982.[43]

These income differences vary regionally. In such chronically poor areas as Ningxia and Gansu, a significant number of peasant families subsist on an average annual per capita income of less than 100 *yuan*.[44] At the same time, in such prosperous areas as Shanghai and Guangzhou, annual per capita incomes of 1000 and even 2500 *yuan* earned

Table 10
Cadre Grades and Salaries

Grade	Position	Monthly Wages (Yuan)
1	Chairman, CCP; General Secretary	540-580
2-3	Premier, Vice-Premier, Standing Committee of Politburo Central Committee	460-540
4-9	Minister, Vice-minister, Provincial Governor, Vice-governor, Party 1st Secretary, 2d Secretary, Department Chief (National)	245-460
10-16	Vice-department Chief, Provincial department chief, Bureau chief, Vice-bureau chief, County Magistrate, Vice-magistrate	110-245
17-22	Section and bureau workers and chiefs	60-110
23-26	Workers and service personnel	33-60
27-30	Workers and apprentices*	23-33

SOURCE: Derived from Jan Prybyla, The Chinese Economy: Problems and Policies, 2d ed. (Columbia: University of South Carolina Press, 1981); Richard Curt Kraus, Class Conflict in Chinese Communism (New York: Columbia University Press, 1981), p. 186; Larry M. Wortzel, "Incentive Mechanisms and Remuneration in China: Policies of the Eleventh Central Committee," Asian Survey 21 (September 1981):974.

*Various accounts state that these grades were eliminated. All grades and wages are a compilation; the Chinese government has not published a wage scale.

from sideline and agricultural production are no longer uncommon.[45] The availability of urban markets and the individual and household responsibility systems in agriculture have contributed to these marked differences in income distribution. Reportedly one model county in Henan province saw increases over earlier years' agricultural grain production of 20 percent in 1979, 37 percent in 1980, and 75 percent in 1981.[46] However, after the allegations about the falsification of production data after the Great Leap Forward and at Dazhai, one must exercise considerable caution in accepting the "new truth" about model production units.

Table 11
Average Per Capita Net Incomes for Workers and Peasants

Source of wages*	1979	1982
People's Communes	85.9	270.0
Workers and Staffs (avg.)	762.0	798.0
Derived from:		
- State owned units	(803.0)	(836.0)
- Collectively owned units	(624.0)	(671.0)

SOURCE: 1979 data - China Daily (Beijing) May 21, 1981; 1982 data - BR no. 19 (May 9, 1983):XI.

*In Ren Min Bi

Table 12
Percentage Distribution of Annual Average Per Capita Income Among Peasant Families

	1982	1983
Over 500 yuan	6.7%	11.9%
150 - 500 yuan	82.5%	80.5%
Under 150 yuan	10.8%	7.6%

SOURCE: BR no. 21 (May 21, 1984):9.

INCOME AND EDUCATION

The income differences between urban and rural areas translate into differences in educational opportunities as well.[47] The reinstitution of an examination system for university admission has emphasized merit over political background, but Party committees (and family relationships) are still deeply involved in the selection process.[48] Because rural production units and townships lack the resources for running quality educational programs, and because keypoint universities select students from keypoint middle schools, orthodox social class (relation-

Table 13
Net Income Per Capita in the Peasant's Household and its Sources (in yuan/RMB)

	1978	1979	1980	1981
Average net income per capita	133.57	160.17	191.33	223.44
Income from the collective	88.53	101.97	108.37	116.20
Income from family sideline production of which:	35.79	44.00	62.55	84.52
- farming and forestry products	15.15	15.29	21.93	28.82
- livestocks, poultry, small animals	12.01	19.00	25.71	33.03
- family handicrafts	1.42	1.76	2.87	3.75
- gathering, fishing, hunting	5.19	3.90	5.80	6.16
- others	2.02	4.05	6.24	12.76
Other incomes besides debit	9.25	14.20	20.41	22.72

SOURCE: Heiner Durr, "Regional Inequalities of Rural Incomes Under the Influence of the Modernization Programme," Paper presented at the Conference on Development and Distribution in China; Centre of Asian Studies, University of Hong Kong, March 14-17, 1983.

ship to the means of production) may be as important as geography in influencing access to education.[49] In this keypoint system key primary and middle schools, often located in areas where there are more cadre or intellectuals, get better teachers, better texts, and larger budgets.[50] As one might imagine, this translates into higher examination scores for admission into secondary schools and universities. Most of the key secondary schools are located in county seats; consequently the further a village is from an urban or market area, the fewer the educational opportunities available to its residents.[51]

The sharp difference in income between rural and urban areas, reduced benefits from collective economic units compared to state-owned units, and narrower access to education put the peasant at a distinct social disadvantage in comparison to the urban worker. Recent changes in the agricultural responsibility system offer the peasant a far greater degree of self-determination than the industrial worker.[52] Nonetheless, the peasant, like the industrial worker, must still tailor production to the requirements imposed by the state planning system. There is no power or authority in self-management, but the peasant may take personal responsibility for the success or failure of a crop.[53]

Peasant markets—and sideline personal businesses for urban workers—may provide greater income, but this does not lead to increased political influence. Likewise, the small private traders in the cities are in no position to articulate their aggregate political interests as a class. Only the Party may broker political interest.

CONCLUSION

In the course of this research we have examined the concept of class from different perspectives: the historical context of the term in the Chinese universe of understanding; the orthodox Marxist understanding of the term; the official position held by the CCP; the popular perception of the concept embodied in literature; and the charges by the dissident Socialist Democracy Movement that the CCP was a "new class." This approach was predicated on two assumptions. First, class in China must be understood through the symbolic universe of Chinese Marxism. Second, an explanation of political reality in China could be applied to other Marxist-Leninist states.[54]

From the outset of the review of the relevant literature, it was apparent that analysis of the legal ownership of the means of production in the socialist state may conform to Marx's definition of class, but *it is not as important for understanding the articulation of aggregate political interest* as it is in the capitalist state. (And for Marx, that was the crux of the analysis—classes must be vehicles for the articulation of political interest). Indeed, there may be no connection between class and interest articulation in China. In order to reflect actual practice in socialist states under communist rule, Marxist theory must be revised to analyze the forms of authority embodied in the control (functional ownership) of the means of production. Hence, borrowing the concept of "economic ownership" from Erik O. Wright, we have been able to characterize the form of control over the means of production exercised by senior enterprise managers (who are most often also senior CCP members).

The CCP has a monopoly of control over the means of production through the authority to make policy in Party committees and through Party influence over enterprise managers. This is not necessarily negative, as such control has enabled the Party to consolidate rapidly after the revolution and to feed, clothe, educate, and provide medical care for a billion people in a systematic manner. However, Party members are the economic owners of the means of production—particularly senior Party leaders in enterprises. This is primarily because the Party dominates enterprise management and the state planning process. But what does this tell us about the Party as it relates to the concept of a "new class?"[55] Is the Party a "new class" as the term is meant by Milovan Djilas, or is it a stratum of society, a privileged ruling elite, as suggested by the Li Yi Zhe Manifesto?[56]

The response in dissident and popular literature is that the concept of class has lost its salience; alientation and self-determination are the two issues undermining Party legitimacy, and the Party must address these issues. Indeed all recent reforms in management and ownership may be seen as attempts to correct these problems.

The CCP draws its members from workers, peasants, and intellectuals (figure 3). The state bureaucracy and the technical bureaucracy of enterprise managers may also contribute members to the Party. Likewise, workers, peasants, or intellectuals may move into positions of leadership in the state or technical bureaucracy; however, this does not necessarily entail Party membership. There are parallels between this open access to the Party and the access to the central bureaucracy in traditional Chinese society. Indeed, the ideological requirements for membership, combined with the access to positions of power afforded by Party membership, seem to have created an elite culture with its own ethos, which perpetuates its own rule.

The special privileges provided offspring of CCP members even mirror those of the old Chinese bureaucrat. The Party provides specific leadership instruction for its initiates; has its own examination system, news propaganda, and cultural organs; even its own system of censor in the Central Discipline Inspection Commission. Party members may reconstitute themselves ideologically by educating and inducting new members and they may pass along certain privileges to their families, but there is no guarantee that Party membership and economic ownership may be passed along to their children.

CCP membership provides a route for access to an improved life-

Figure 3
Access to the Ruling Elite

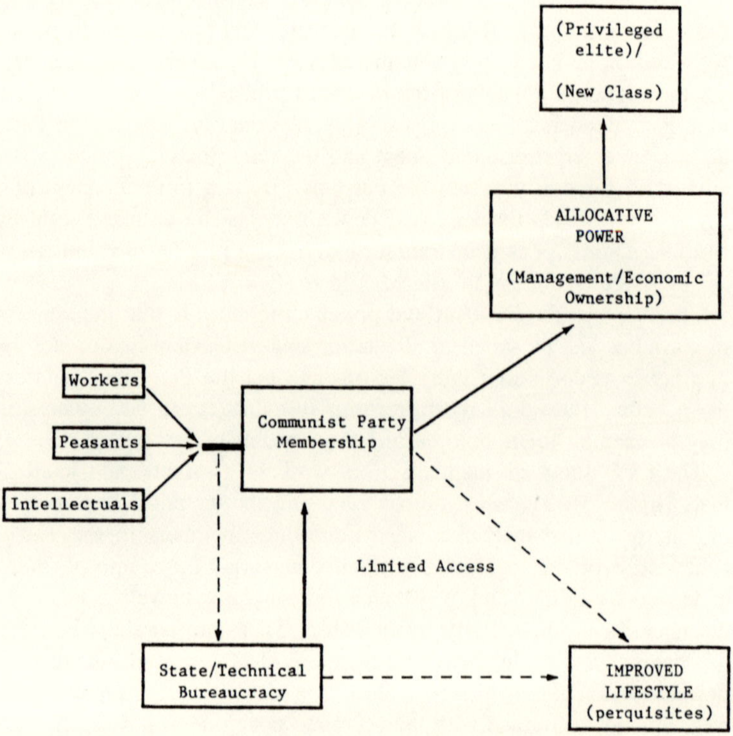

style and certain perquisites, but it is only a necessary condition for such access and not a sufficient condition. Many Party members remain in jobs among peasants or workers and continue to do grassroots political work. Although some Party members enjoy access to such perquisites as telephones, automobiles, and improved living conditions, these things are increasingly becoming available to the general populace. Only select Party members move into positions where they may control the allocation of commodities, housing, or work—acting as economic owners of the means of production. Because all citizens of the socialist state in China jointly own the state-controlled means of production, they may be said to form strata of a larger unitary class composed of the entire citizenry. Even those people employed in collective enterprises, who invest in the new stock market, or those who own individual businesses are members of this unitary class because they also share legal ownership of the state enterprises. What does this mean for class analysis in China?

A Marxian analysis of class in China has permitted a more complete examination of differences in income, living conditions, and educational opportunities as they relate to the ownership of the means of production. However, Marx intended the concept to be of some use in describing the relationship between ownership and the allocation and control of products of labor. Instead, political power in China is more closely related to the authority of the ruling vanguard party and its control of the state planning process. The CCP enjoys unidimensional control of the superstructure and the economic base. As conceptual language, the term ''class'' is near bankrupt to analyze political economy in socialist states. To analyze political economy in socialist states one must employ the concepts of interest and economic ownership.

Sectoral Interests Versus Class Interests

The concept of class has been used for factional struggles that have torn the fabric of Chinese society, causing the term ''class'' to summon images of narrow Party interest rather than aggregrate political interest for workers or peasants. We are left with a concept that cannot describe politico-economic reality in China.

Political power in the socialist state is related to the level of authority to which one rises in the Communist Party, but that fact does nothing to illuminate political pressures in the socialist state. Party bureaucrats must still respond to, or repress with psychological or physical force, the protests or pressures coming from sectors of the economy. Peasants, workers in heavy or light industry, transport workers, and the like have a set of interests related to their means of employment. How is the production quota allocated? What industries may send students to foreign colleges? What industries may undertake capital construction?

These sectoral pressures have a ''stovepipe'' (or vertical) effect, relating political and economic interest vertically in the sector of the economy in which an individual is employed. Although there is a general convergence of interests among all workers toward the goal of obtaining some measure of autonomy and self-determination in the planning and allocative processes, this autonomy is obtained only through the good graces of some intervening level of Party organization—enterprise, local, provincial, or national. The result of these pressures is that social "class," as a relationship to the means of production, has lost meaning.

Vertical, hierarchical interests in the economic sectors are the constituent elements of political interest in China. These interests relate to wealth, decisionmaking, the expansion of employment opportunities, housing, and so on. These interests are represented by the state bureaucracy through its ministries, bureaus, and regional offices, and struggles over who gets what are fought among economic sectors. The Party sets the guiding policies for such decisions and at the same time is heavily represented in the senior ranks of government.

Ruling Elites and Interest Articulation

That at its higher echelons the CCP constitutes a ruling elite is true, but what language have we to characterize that elite? We are faced with a political party that legitimizes its continued existence and dominance by its own claim to ordained historical transience in the future. The CCP has done much for China, but the human price paid for these improvements has been great. Much of the stratified relationship between the Party and the populace, through the bureaucracy, reflects the continuation of traditional Chinese bureaucratic society. Despite recurrent efforts to purge itself of those cadre who abuse their position, the Party's legitimacy remains threatened. Most seriously, the Party has reacted to attempts to develop a new critical language as an effort to understand stratification in China by the arrest and repression of those who worked to create new forms of meaning.

The existence of an elite structure is a direct result of the Party's self-legitimating authority through the doctrine of democratic centralism. This doctrine not only stifles dissent, which would illuminate the problems in society, but also avoids acknowledging that the very hegemony of the system presents a problem. The baggage from political mass movements, from class struggles, and from the Cultural Revolution has undermined the concepts used in Marxian class analysis in

China. A new paradigm must be developed that accounts for the hierarchical stratification of socialist society.

The political pressures brought to bear on the CCP and the Chinese state through government ministries must be more fully explored. Future thinking should focus on the articulation of interests between different sectors of the economy. As economic sectors seek to articulate their interests through the ministries and in the Party they exert political influence and pressure. The nature of state planning and the requirement for democratic centralism makes the vertical authority inherent in the sector the only legitimate vehicle for expression. The reaction to the 1986-1987 demonstrations for more freedom shows that any attempt to undertake collective political action will be quashed. Political action is tolerated only through the established Party-approved structures. Different sectors of the economy, as a result of their representatives, will receive more or less influence in the economic development and allocation process. Political life in China should be explored through this system of state planning, enterprise, and macroeconomic management to understand more completely how political interest is articulated.

Notes

CHAPTER 1

1. Notable exceptions to this are Rudolf Bahro, *The Alternative in Eastern Europe* (Manchester: New Left Books, 1978); Zygmunt Bauman, "Officialdom and Class: Bases of Inequality in Socialist Society," in *The Social Analysis of Class Structure*, ed. Frank Parkin (London: Tavistock Publishers, 1974), pp. 129–148; Leszek Kolakowski, *Main Currents of Marxism*, vol. 3: *The Breakdown* (Oxford: Clarendon Press, 1978); Jaroslav Krejci, *Social Change and Stratification in Postwar Czechoslovakia* (New York: Columbia University Press, 1972); Mihailo Markovic, *From Affluence to Praxis* (Ann Arbor: University of Michigan Press, 1974); Wang Xizhe, "For a Return to Genuine Marxism in China," *New Left Review* 121 (May 1980):33–48.

2. Milovan Djilas, *The New Class* (New York: Holt, Rinehart and Winston, 1957), pp. 39–69.

3. See Wang Xizhe, "For a Return to Genuine Marxism in China," pp. 33–48; Li Yizhe, "Guanyu shehui zhuyi de minzhu yu fazhi) [On the socialist democratic and legal system]," in *Minzhu zhonghua* [Democratic China], ed. Xianggang zhongwen daxue (Hong Kong: Zhongwen daxue, 1983), pp. 53–82.

4. On the changes in the commune system see "A Review of Current Agricultural Policies in China," Economic Section, American Consulate General, Hong Kong (October 14, 1983); Tang Tsou, Marc Belcher, and Mitch Meisner, "The Responsibility System in Agriculture," *Modern China* 8, no. 1 (January 1982):41–103.

5. Here the work of neo-Marxists is instructive. The term "neo-Marxist" denotes the work of contemporary theorists who have applied Marx, with some revision, to advanced industrial societies. The major industries in such societies are generally publicly owned corporations that remain capitalist. However, the ownership of the means of production in these industries is so widely shared that different classes may have mutual interests in the industry. Some examples are Rosemary Crompton and John Gubbay, *Economy and Class Structure* (New York: St. Martin's Press, 1978); Ralph Miliband, *The State in Capitalist Society* (London: Weidenfeld and Nicholson, 1969); Nicos Poulantzas, *Political Power and Social Classes* (London: New Left Books, 1973); idem, *State, Power, Socialism* (London: New Left Books, 1978); Erik O. Wright, *Class, Crisis, and the State* (London: New Left Books, 1978).

6. The work of the Frankfurt School of critical theorists is particularly important for an explanation of the subjugation of workers to the state. See Jürgen Habermas, *Knowledge and Human Interests* (Boston: Beacon Press, 1971). Also see E. P. Thompson, *The Poverty of Theory and Other Essays* (London: Monthly Review Press, 1978); Paul Ricoeur, "The Model of the Text: Meaningful Action Considered as Text," in Paul Rabinow and William N. Sullivan, *Interpretive Social Science: A Reader* (Berkeley: University of California Press, 1979), pp. 73–102; Leo Strauss, *What Is Political Philosophy?* (New York: Free Press, 1959); idem, *The City and Man* (Chicago: Rand McNally, 1964).

7. Some readings on the rules for exegesis, or interpretive analysis, are Zygmunt Bauman, *Hermeneutics and Social Science: Approaches to Understanding* (London: Hutchinson, 1978); Paul Connerton, *Critical Sociology: Selected Readings* (New York: Penguin Books, 1976); Jürgen Habermas, *Theory and Practice* (Boston: Beacon Press, 1974); Hans Kung and Jürgen Moltmann, *Conflicting Ways of Interpreting the Bible* (New York: Seabury Press, 1980); Richard E. Palmer, *Hermeneutics: Interpretation Theory in Schleiermacher, Dilthey, Heidegger, and Gadamer* (Evanston: Northwestern University Press, 1969); Paul Ricoeur, *The Conflict of Interpretations: Essays in Hermeneutics* (Evanston: Northwestern University Press, 1974); and Ricoeur, *Freud and Philosophy: An Essay on Interpretation*, trans. Dennis Savage (New Haven: Yale University Press, 1978).

8. Ricoeur, *Freud and Philosophy*, pp. 8–9, 24–26.

9. Ibid., p. 8.

10. Ibid., p. 24. Also see Habermas, *Theory and Practice*, pp. 18–19; and Michael J. Shapiro, *Language and Political Understanding: The Politics of Discursive Practices* (New Haven: Yale University Press, 1981).

11. Ricoeur, *Freud and Philosophy*, p. 25.

12. The forms of "methods" texts to which I refer are Charles H. Backstrum and Gerald D. Hursh, *Survey Research* (Evanston: Northwestern Uni-

versity Press, 1963); Johan Galtung, *Theory and Methods of Social Research* (London: George Allen and Unwin, 1967); David G. Garson, *Political Science Methods* (Boston: Holbrook Press, 1976); Arthur L. Stinchcombe, *Constructing Social Theories* (New York: Harcourt Brace and World, 1968). I found the following more useful: William J. Filstead, *Qualitative Methodology: Firsthand Involvement with the Social World* (Chicago: Markham, 1970); and Eugene Webb, Donald Campbell, et al., *Unobtrusive Measures: Non-Reactive Research in the Social Sciences* (Chicago: Rand McNally, 1966).

13. Thompson, *The Poverty of Theory*, pp. 35–39.

14. Edward Schillebeeckx, *Jesus: An Experiment in Christology*, trans. Huber Hoskins (New York: Vintage Books, 1981), p. 48.

15. Palmer, *Hermeneutics: Interpretation Theory*, p. 57.

16. This is the thesis of the introduction to Frank Parkin, *Marxism and Class Theory: A Bourgeois Critique* (New York: Columbia University Press, 1979).

17. I use the term "socialist state" in the sense that Lane does in reference to "state socialism." The dominant values are Marxism-Leninism, the state owns a majority of the means of production, and there is a belief in the ultimate perfectability of people and the determining influence of class struggle in history. David Lane, *The Socialist Industrial State* (Boulder, CO: Westview Press, 1976), p. 13.

18. This comes from discussions with Michael Shapiro. More can be found in chapters five and seven of his book *Language and Political Understanding*. Other references based on this concept are Michel Foucault, *Madness and Civilization* (New York: Pantheon Books, 1965); idem, *The Order of Things: An Archaeology of the Human Sciences* (New York: Vintage Books, 1973), and *The Archaeology of Knowledge* (New York: Harper & Row, 1976).

19. This is Foucault's thesis in *The Archaeology of Knowledge*.

20. See Kolakowski, *Main Currents of Marxism*, vol. 3, passim; Svetozar Stojanovic, *Between Ideals and Reality* (London: Oxford University Press, 1973); Mihailo Markovic and Gado Petrovic, eds., *Praxis* (Boston: D. Reidel, 1979); Markovic, *From Affluence to Praxis*; Djilas, *The New Class*; and Bahro, *The Alternative in Eastern Europe*.

21. I draw on the general description of liberalism by John Dunn, *Western Political Theory in the Face of the Future* (London: Cambridge University Press, 1979), pp. 28–54.

22. Refer to Franz Schurmann, *Ideology and Organization in Communist China*, 2d ed. (Berkeley: University of California Press, 1968).

23. Interview, Hong Kong, March 15, 1983.

24. Robert D. Scalapino, ed., *Elites in the People's Republic of China* (Seattle: University of Washington Press, 1972).

25. Ibid., pp. vi, xviii, 6.

26. Lucian W. Pye, *The Dynamics of Factions and Consensus in Chinese Politics* (Santa Monica: Rand Corporation, 1980).

27. Parris H. Chang, "Chinese Politics: Deng's Turbulent Quest," *Problems of Communism* 30 (January-February 1981):12–31.

28. Richard Curt Kraus, *Class Conflict in Chinese Socialism* (New York: Columbia University Press, 1981).

CHAPTER 2

1. Etienne Balazs, *Chinese Civilization and Bureaucracy* (New York: Yale University Press, 1964), pp. 14–27.

2. Ibid., p. 6.

3. Ibid., p. 16.

4. Donald J. Munro, *The Concept of Man in Early China* (Stanford: Stanford University Press, 1969), p. viii.

5. Ibid., p. 5.

6. John Winthrop Haeger, ed., *Crisis and Prosperity in Sung China* (Tucson: University of Arizona Press, 1975), p. 2.

7. Munro, *Man in Early China*, p. 7.

8. Ibid., p. viii.

9. I have drawn here on concepts introduced in Foucault, *The Archaeology of Knowledge* and *Madness and Civilization*. Foucault suggests that there are rules that must be used to analyze both conduct and language practices—rules that are specific to a society. Furthermore, meanings change over time but are dervied from earlier meanings. See also Shapiro, *Language and Political Understanding*, pp. 127–164; and Hans-Georg Gadamer, *Truth and Method* (New York: Seabury Press, 1975).

10. Plato, "The Republic," in *Great Dialogues of Plato*, trans. W. H. D. Rouse (New York: Mentor Books, 1956), pp. 214–215.

11. Munro, *Man in Early China*, pp. 18–19.

12. Marcel Granet, *Chinese Civilization* (New York: Alfred A. Knopf, 1930), pp. 9–13.

13. Ibid., p. 10.

14. Ibid., pp. 16–17.

15. William McNaughton, ed., *The Confucian Vision* (Ann Arbor: University of Michigan Press, 1974), p. 6.

16. Munro, *Man in Early China*, pp. 18–19.

17. Wolfram Eberhard suggests that traditional (feudal) Chinese society was originally divided into two classes: the nobility and the ruled. The class of persons ruled was divided into strata, including even high officials. See Eberhard, *Conquerors and Rulers: Social Forces in Medieval China*, 2d ed. (Leiden: E. J. Brill, 1970), pp. 23–28; also see Brian C. McKnight, "Fiscal Priv-

ileges and Social Order in Sung China,'' in Haegar, *Crisis and Prosperity in Sung China*, pp. 97–98.

18. Ho Ping-ti, *The Ladder of Success in Imperial China* (New York: Columbia University Press, 1962), pp. 17–18.

19. Donald J. Munro, *The Concept of Man in Contemporary China* (Ann Arbor: University of Michigan Press, 1977), pp. 135–136.

20. Frits Staal, ''Oriental Ideas on the Origin of Language,'' *Journal of the American Oriental Society* 1 (January-March 1979):1–14.

21. T'ang Chun-I, ''The Individual and the World in Chinese Methodology,'' in *The Status of the Individual in East and West*, ed. Charles A. Moore (Honolulu: University of Hawaii Press, 1968), p. 102.

22. Confucius, *The Analects* (Lun yu) 3:8, trans. James Legge (New York: Dover Publications, 1971), pp. 262–264.

23. Munro, *Man in Contemporary China*, p. 135.

24. Ibid., pp. 136–138.

25. Harry Harding, *Organizing China: The Problem of Bureaucracy* (Stanford: Stanford University Press, 1981), pp. 21–24, 43–62, 114–163, 202–234, 309–326.

26. Gong-sun Long, ''Bai ma lun'' [Discussion of a white horse], in *Zhongguo zhexueshi jiaoxue ziliao xuanji* [A Compilation of Teaching Materials on the History of Chinese Philosophy], vol. 1 (Beijing: Zhonghua Shuzhu, 1980), pp. 182–185. Also see Beijing daxue zhexuexi, ed. *Zhongguo zhexueshi* [A History of Chinese Philosophy], vol. 1 (Beijing: Zhonghua shuzhu, 1980), pp. 127–131.

27. Hsun-tzu, *Basic Writings*, trans. Burton Watson (New York: Columbia University Press, 1963), pp. 139–156.

28. Ho, *The Ladder of Success*, pp. 17–18.

29. Ibid., pp. 24–25.

30. Confucius, *Analects* 4:7. This order of *shi*, *nong*, *gong*, *shang* is acknowledged as the accepted class ranking from the establishment of a unified state in China in 221 B.C. through at least the late Qing dynasty. See Joseph R. Levenson, *Confucian China and Its Modern Fate: A Trilogy*, vol. 3 (Berkeley: University of California Press, 1965), pp. 35–38; also see Ho, *The Ladder of Success*, pp. 256–257; and H. G. Creel, *Chinese Thought from Confucius to Mao Tse-tung* (Chicago: University of Chicago Press, 1953).

31. Haegar, *Crisis and Prosperity*, p. 157.

32. Albert Feuerwerker, ''A White Horse May or May Not Be a Horse, but Megahistory Is Not Economic History,'' in *The Development of Underdevelopment in China*, Philip C. C. Huang, ed. (White Plains, N.Y.: M. E. Sharpe, 1980), pp. 81–89.

33. Balazs, *Chinese Civilization and Bureaucracy*, pp.6–7.

34. Ibid.

35. Ibid.

36. Eberhard, *Conquerors and Rulers*, p. 42.

37. Ho, *The Ladder of Success*, pp. 17–28.

38. Balazs, *Chinese Civilization and Bureaucracy*, pp. 14–16.

39. The individual's class status must be conceived in terms of the family according to Eberhard, *Conquerors and Rulers*, p. 20.

40. T'ung-tsu Ch'u, "China's Class Structure and Its Ideology," in *Chinese Thought and Institutions*, John K. Fairbank, ed. (Chicago: University of Chicago Press, 1951), pp. 235–250.

41. Fei Hsiao-t'ung, *China's Gentry* (Chicago: University of Chicago Press, 1953), pp. 9–27.

42. Ho, *The Ladder of Success*, p. 19.

43. Ibid., pp. 19–35.

44. Arthur F. Wright and Dennis Twitchett, eds., *Confucian Personalities* (Stanford: Stanford University Press, 1962), p. 11.

45. T'ung-tsu Ch'u, *Han Social Structure*, ed. by Jack L. Dull (Seattle: University of Washington Press, 1972), pp. 63–64.

46. Ibid., p. 66.

47. Eberhard, *Conquerors and Rulers*, pp. 42–43, 159–160. Eberhard notes that the class of a family was entered into official records in the tenth century A.D. Only a legal act could change a family's class, lending a castelike nature to social stratification.

48. Chang Chung-li, *The Chinese Gentry* (Seattle: University of Washington Press, 1955), pp. 3–10. Chang bases his analysis of Chinese ruling elites on local histories that were often written on commission from a senior official in an area. Also see Ho Ping-ti's *Ladder of Success*, which Ho claims is less biased because it is based on research over three successive generations of imperial examination booklets and results.

49. Munro, *Man in Early China*, pp. 8–9.

50. McKnight, "Fiscal Privileges and Social Order," pp. 97–98.

51. Karl A. Wittfogel, *Oriental Despotism* (New Haven: Yale University Press, 1957), pp. 79–81, 116.

52. Fei, *China's Gentry*, pp. 17–19, 31–32.

53. Ch'u, *Han Social Structure*, chap. 4.

54. C. K. Yang, *A Chinese Village in Early Communist Transition*, 2 vols. (Cambridge: MIT Press, 1959), pp. 6–7, 119–127.

55. Munro, *Man in Contemporary China*, p. 17.

56. Ibid., pp. 134–148.

57. H. G. Creel, "The Beginnings of Bureaucracy in China: The Origin of the Hsien," *Journal of Asian Studies* 23 (February 1964):155–184.

58. Levenson, *Confucian China and Its Modern Past*, passim.

CHAPTER 3

1. My purpose is not a detailed exegesis of Mao's works. For that type of treatment the reader may refer to the following: Donald J. Munro, *The Concept of Man in Contemporary China* (Ann Arbor: University of Michigan Press, 1977); Stuart R. Schram, *The Political Thought of Mao Tse-tung* (New York: Praeger Publishers, 1963); Benjamin I. Schwartz, *Chinese Communism and the Rise of Mao* (Cambridge: Harvard University Press, 1951); Frederic Wakeman, Jr., *History and Will: Philosophical Perspectives of Mao Tse-tung's Thought* (Berkeley: University of California Press, 1973); Andrew G. Walder, "Marxism, Maoism, and Social Change," *Modern China* 3, nos. 1–2 (1977):101–118, 125–160. I will avoid the argument over whether Mao has provided any distinctly original new thought as a contribution to Marxism; the subject is outside the scope of this book. On this question the reader may refer to Wakeman, *History and Will*, pp. 295–296 and Schram, *Political Thought of Mao*, pp. 308–316. My discussion will be limited to efforts to understand how Mao differentiated classes in China in order to use the epistemology as a basis for explicating the official position regarding class held by the CCP.

2. Chinese Communist Party (CCP), "Resolution on Certain Questions in the History of Our Party since the Founding of the People's Republic of China," in *Resolution on CPC History* (Beijing: Foreign Languages Press, 1981), pp. 56–73. I will not utilize all of the texts mentioned in the "Resolution" but will concentrate on those texts used in political study and reeducation sessions in China that, according to two of the informants I have interviewed, are particularly important. I will cite Mao's *Selected Works* as *SW*, and have also provided the page numbers from the Chinese edition in brackets following the English citation. When necessary to remain consistent with the original title of a published work, I use the Wade-Giles romanization system.

3. The major texts utilized are Mao Zedong, "Analysis of Classes in Chinese Society," *Selected Works of Mao Tse-tung*, vol. 1 (Beijing: Foreign Languages Press, 1975), pp. 13–22 [3–11]; "How to Differentiate the Classes in Rural Areas," *SW*, 1:137–140 [121–124]; "On Practice," *SW*, 1:295–310 [271–286]; "On Contradiction," *SW*, 1:311–345 [287–306]; "Report on the Investigation of the Peasant Movement in Hunan," *SW*, I:23–59 [13–46]; "The Tasks of the Chinese Communist Party in the Period of Resistance to Japan," *SW*, 1:263–283 [243–260]; "The Role of the Chinese Communist Party in the National War," *SW*, 2:195–211 [507–524]; "On New Democracy," *SW*, 2:339–384 [655–704]; "Rectify the Party's Style of Work," *SW*, 3:35–51 [813–830]; "Talks at the Yanan Forum on Literature and Art," *SW*, 3:69–98 [849–880]; "On the Question of the National Bourgeoisie and Enlightened Gentry," *SW*, 4:207–210 [1285–1299]; "On the People's Demo-

cratic Dictatorship,'' *SW*, 4:411–424 [1473–1486]; ''On the Ten Major Relationships,'' *SW*, 5:284–307 [267–288]; ''On the Correct Handling of Contradictions among the People,'' *SW*, 5:384–421 [363–402].

4. I have reviewed sixteen texts used by Beijing University, Nanjing University, and Hangzhou University that are listed separately in the bibliography under ''educational materials.'' I developed my interpretation of this epistemology through the review of those texts, a reading of Mao's works and Party commentary on them, and lengthy discussions with three Chinese intellectuals. One of the informants is a former Party cadre who attended the Anti-Japanese Military and Political College at Yanan. All three of the informants underwent ''reeducation'' at the hands of the Party during which they were forced to memorize the works of Mao and Party commentaries on them.

5. Karl Marx, ''The Eighteenth Brumaire of Louis Bonaparte,'' in Karl Marx and Frederick Engels, *Selected Works*, vol. 1 (Moscow: Progress Publishers, 1969), pp. 421–423, 442–443, 474–487.

6. A mode of production is related to a given historical period and is a combination of forces of production, social relations of production, and the instruments (means) of production. Karl Marx, *Capital*, 3 vols. (New York: Vintage Books, 1981), 1:505, 617, 1064–1066.

7. Herbert Marcuse, *Soviet Marxism* (New York: Columbia University Press, 1958), pp. 21–25; Georg Lukacs, *History and Class Consciousness*, trans. Rodney Livingstone (Cambridge: MIT Press, 1971), pp. 46–82.

8. Marx, *Capital*, 1:284–285.

9. Ibid., 3:1025–1026.

10. Karl Marx and Frederick Engels, ''Feuerbach: Opposition of the Materialistic and Idealistic Outlook,'' in *Selected Works*, 1:65.

11. Marcuse, *Soviet Marxism*, p. 41.

12. I have avoided a detailed discussion of the state, but the concept of class in Marxism-Leninism is so tied to the institution of the state that some mention is necessary. See Vladimir I. Lenin, ''State and Revolution,'' in Arthur P. Mandel, ed. *The Essential Works of Marxism* (New York: Bantam Books, 1961), pp. 103–206. Lenin's formula of the vanguard was a political strategy of elitism. He suggests a disregard for the sensitivities and intelligence of the ''masses'' in general, declaring that only an intellectual elite of dedicated revolutionaries can develop a political consciousness among workers. See Lenin, ''What Is to Be Done?'' in *Collected Works*, vol. 5 (Moscow: Progress Publishers, 1973), especially pp. 78–79. Contrast his disregard for the masses with the treatment given working classes in Barrington Moore, *Injustice: The Social Basis of Obedience and Revolt* (White Plains, N.Y.: M. E. Sharpe, 1978), and the treatment of the peasant in James C. Scott, *The Moral Economy of the Peasant* (New Haven: Yale University Press, 1976).

13. V. I. Lenin, "A Great Beginning," in *Essentials of Lenin*, 3 vols. (London: Lawrence and Wishart, 1949), 2:492.

14. Lenin, "State and Revolution," p. 104.

15. Ibid., p. 105.

16. Ibid., pp. 104–105; Mervyn Mathews, *Class and Society in Soviet Russia* (New York: Penguin Press, 1972), p. 34.

17. Josef Stalin, Speech to the Eighth Congress of the Soviets, November 25, 1936. Excerpts of the speech may be found in Mathews, *Class and Society*, p. 41, and *RMRB*, March 9, 1982. Note that in *RMRB* Stalin's theory is categorized as a "theory from abroad," and Mao's essays are praised as more appropriate for Chinese society.

18. I have paraphrased Stalin's speech here.

19. The "Yanan Spirit" for Party members is characterized by the self-reliant nature of life at the guerrilla base between the years 1936 and 1948, a lack of concern for personal comfort, and a willingness to work hard. It has also been called the "Yanan work style" (Yanan zuofeng). See *RMRB*, January 15, 1961; *RMRB*, August 23, 1975; and Mark Selden, *The Yenan Way in Revolutionary China* (Cambridge: Harvard University Press, 1971).

20. Richard Curt Kraus, *Class Conflict in Chinese Socialism* (New York: Columbia University Press, 1981), p. 28.

21. Ibid., 27–28.

22. John Bryan Starr, *Continuing the Revolution: The Political Thought of Mao* (Princeton: Princeton University Press, 1979), pp. 98, 99–116.

23. Kraus, *Class Conflict in Chinese Socialism*, p. 20, makes reference to the method Mao relied upon to distinguish classes. However, Kraus does not focus on it as an explanation for what he sees as "confusion" over the concept of class by the CCP.

24. Mao, *SW*, 1:13 [3–4].

25. Ibid.

26. Ibid., p. 19 [8–9].

27. Mao, "Analysis of Classes in Chinese Society," *SW* 1:26–28, 34–39 [16–18, 23–29]; "How to Differentiate the Classes in Rural Areas," passim.

28. Mao condemns the supernatural system of traditional Chinese religion and what he calls the "superstitious and feudal" traditional political system in *SW*, 1:44–47 [33–37]. Feudal thought remains an ill-defined category. However, implicit in all references to feudalism by Mao is a reliance on interrelationships and communication based upon the recognition of positions of superiority or inferiority stemming from traditional patriarchal society. The entire Confucian system is implicated . See Confucius, *The Analects*, passim.; Wittfogel, *Oriental Despotism*, pp. 414–418, considers that an essential element of feudal society in China is "a strict attachment of the peasant to his

land or village.'' The term ''feudal'' is used by Hinton to describe a system where a ruling class, basing its power on the private ownership of and control over land, lived off a share of the produce extracted from that land by a class of laboring people . . . so closely bound to the land they cultivated as to make them little better than serfs of the landed proprietors''; William Hinton, *Fanshen: A Documentary of Revolution in a Chinese Village* (New York: Vintage Books, 1966), p. 26 fn.

29. Mao, ''Analysis of Classes,'' p. 19.

30. Hinton, *Fanshen*, pp. 229–231.

31. Wakeman, *History and Will*, p. 38.

32. Mao, *SW*, 1:13 [3]. Note that class is always conceived as existing in a state of tension with another class. See Kraus, *Class Conflict*, pp. 46–50. Kraus, however, because he focuses so deeply on the question of conflict and struggle, never comes to terms with how classes are conceived and analyzed by Party members. As I shall argue, the reification of social relations into exclusive, antithetical elements that is characteristic of Party thought contributes to new selections of objects for struggle by the Party.

33. This approach by Mao is theoretically consistent with Marx and Engels. See ''Feuerbach: Opposition of the Materialistic and Idealistic Outlook,'' p. 47.

34. Mao, *SW*, 1:14–15 [4–5].

35. Hinton, *Fanshen*, pp. 34–35.

36. Mao, *SW*, 1:16–17 [6–7].

37. Ibid., *SW*, 1:137–139 [121–123].

38. Ibid., p. 138 [123].

39. Interview with a PRC defector in the United States.

40. Hinton, *Fanshen*, pp. 436–437.

41. Mao, *SW*, 1:16–17 [6–7].

42. Ibid., p. 19 [8–9].

43. Ibid., p. 18 [7–8], 1:139 [123].

44. Schram, *The Political Thought of Mao*, pp. 172–177.

45. Mao, *SW*, 1:19 [8–9].

46. Mao, *SW*, 4:207 [1285].

47. Ibid., p. 209 [1287–1288].

48. Mao, *SW*, 1:295–296, 311 [272, 288].

49. Schurmann, *Ideology and Organization in Communist China*, p. 53.

50. *RMRB*, December 26, 1983. Wu Jiang, *Guanyu yanjiu Mao Zedong zhexue sixiang di jige wenti* [Several Questions with Regard to the Study of Mao Zedong's Philosophical Thought] (Beijing: Beijing chubanshe, 1982), pp. 6–7.

51. Ibid., p. 13; idem, *Renshilun shijiang* [Ten Lectures on Epistemology] (Shanghai: Renmin chubanshe), pp. 58–59.

52. *RMRB*, July, 1986.

53. Mao, *SW*, 1:295 [271].

54. Ibid., pp. 296–297 [273].

55. Ibid., p. 306 [283].

56. Ibid., p. 308 [285]. For a more detailed discussion of Mao's theories on practice see Starr, "On Knowing and Doing," in *Continuing the Revolution*, pp. 46–71.

57. Mao, *SW*, 1:306 [283].

58. Ibid., 1:316 [292–293].

59. Ibid., p. 317, 338 [293, 316].

60. Starr, *Continuing the Revolution*, pp. 3–8.

61. Lao Tsu, "Tao Teh King" [Pinyin latinization: Dao De Jing], in *The Texts of Taoism*, trans. James Legge (New York: Dover Publications, 1962), pp. 47–48.

62. Richard Wilhelm, *The I-Ching: Or Book of Changes*, trans. Cary F. Baynes, 3d ed. (Princeton: Princeton University Press, 1967).

63. Levenson, *Modern China and Its Confucian Past*, p. 210, also cited in Baum, "Science and Culture in Contemporary China," p. 1169.

64. See Mao, *SW*, 1:315–330 [292–308]. For a detailed analysis refer to Ai Hengwu and Lin Qingshan, "Yi fen wei er yu he er er yi" [One Dividing into Two and Two Combining into One], *GMRB*, May 29, 1964. Also see *RMRB*, November 1, 1967; Wu Jiang, *Guanyu yanjiu Mao Zedong siziang*, pp. 26–28.

65. *GMRB*, May 29, 1964.

66. Mao, *SW*, 1:344–345 [323–324].

67. Ibid., p. 345 [324].

68. Mao, *SW*, vol. 5.

69. Schurmann, *Ideology and Organization*, pp. 53–54, 55.

70. Mao, *SW*, 5:385–387 [364–365].

71. Ibid., p. 385 [364].

72. Ibid.

73. Xiao Wu, "Xuexi jieji fenxi fangfa" [Study the Method of Class Analysis], *Xin jianshe* (February 1952):17–18.

74. Fu Suilan, "Du: Zhongguo shehui ge jieji de fenxi" [Read: An analysis of the Classes in Chinese Society], *Xin jianshe* (February 1952):19–21.

75. Kraus, *Class Conflict*, pp. 115–141.

76. Ibid., pp. 185–187. Also see Frances Lai Fung-wai, "Contradictions among Personal Status, Family Status, and the Concept of Class in the People's Republic of China," paper prepared for the Association for Asian Studies Conference, Gainesville, Florida, January 20–23, 1977 (typewritten), pp. 7–10.

77. See Hinton, *Fanshen*, pp. 401–410, 434–475, 548–550. The process

of "capping" is described in Martin King Whyte, "Inequality and Stratification in China," *The China Quarterly* 64 (October 1975):684–711; and Gordon White, *The Politics of Class and Class Origin: The Case of the Cultural Revolution* (Canberra: Contemporary China Centre, Australian National University, 1976).

78. Hua Guofeng, *Continue the Revolution under the Dictatorship of the Proletariat to the End* (Beijing: Foreign Languages Press, 1977), p. 20.

79. Ibid., pp. 20–22.

80. Ye Jianying, *Speech at the Meeting in Celebration of the Founding of the 30th Anniversary of the People's Republic of China* (September 29, 1979) (Beijing: Foreign Languages Press, 1979), pp. 44–45.

81. Ibid., pp. 8–9.

82. Xu Dixin, "Lun woguo guomin jingji de biange yu fazhan" [A Discussion of the Transformation and Development of China's National Economy], in *Shehuizhuyi zhengzhi jingjixue ruogan jiben lilun wenti* (Jinan: Shandong chubanshe, 1980), pp. 14–16.

83. Surprisingly, a librarian let me check it out for a few days. He never checked the caveat.

84. Zhongguo shehui kexueyuan qingbao yanjiusou, *Sulian lilun jielun shehui zhuyi shehui de jieji* [Boundaries of Soviet Theoretical Discussions of Class in Socialist Society] (Beijing: Zhongguo shehui kexueyuan chubanshe, 1980).

85. Ibid., pp. 1–3.

86. Ibid., p. 21.

87. Ibid., p. 22.

88. Ibid., pp. 21–25.

89. Ibid., p. 21.

90. Ibid., p. 24.

91. Ibid., p. 43.

92. This analysis of Soviet society is supported by the evaluations of eleven Soviet scholars with whom I attended the National University of Singapore.

93. Nicholas Lardy, ed., *Chinese Economic Planning: Translations of Chi-Hua Ching-chi* (White Plains, N.Y.: M. E. Sharpe, 1977–1978), pp. 122–124. Also see Xue Muqiao, *China's Socialist Economy* (Beijing: Foreign Languages Press, 1981), pp. 45–66, 266–288; Sun Yuefang, *Shehui zhuyi jingji di ruogan lilun wenti* [Basic theoretical questions of the socialist economy] (Wuhan: Renmin chubanshe, 1982), pp. 209–226.

94. I am indebted to an article criticizing "traditional" epistemology for opening my eyes to the change from epistemology to ideology in the Maoist theory of knowledge. See W. Suchting, "Knowledge and Practice: Towards a Marxist Critique of Traditional Epistemology," *Science and Society* 47 (Spring 1983):2–36.

95. Constitution of the Communist Party of China (Adopted by the Twelfth National Congress on September 6, 1982), "General Programme," p. 3.

96. Ibid.

97. *GMRB*, September 7, 1982.

98. Shanghai *JFRB*, December 5, 1979.

99. *Jiefangjun bao* is a publication of the People's Liberation Army. This was broadcast in China by the Beijing Domestic Service. A translation of the full text of the commentary appears in Foreign Broadcast Information Service—China-(FBIS-CHI)82-197 (October 12, 1982):K1–K8.

100. Ibid., p. K5.

101. Ibid., pp. K6–K7.

102. Yu Yannan, "Guanyu woguo zichan jieji zuowei boxue jieji xiaomie yihou di gongren jieji" [On the Working Class after the Elimination of the Bourgeoisie as an Exploiting Class in Our Country] *Hong Qi* 16 (August 16, 1982):14–18.

103. Ibid., pp. 15–16.

104. Ibid., p. 18.

105. On the "San Fan Yun Dong" [Three-Anti Movement] against corruption waste and bureaucracy in the Party see *RMRB*, December 15, 1951, December 31, 1951, and December 10, 1953. On the redefinition of class and the campaign to turn criminals into class enemies see *RMRB*, November 6, 1982; U.S. Joint Publications Research Service (JPRS) No. 81788 (September 16, 1982):56–59.

CHAPTER 4

1. Merle Goldman, *Literary Dissent in Communist China* (New York: Atheneum Press, 1971), p. 1.

2. Ibid.

3. See Chow Tse-tsung, *The May Fourth Movement: Intellectual Revolution in Modern China* (Cambridge: Harvard University Press, 1960); Mao Zedong, "The May Fourth Movement," *SW*, 2:237–239; idem, "On New Democracy," *SW*, 3:369–382.

4. Chow, *The May Fourth Movement*, pp. 20–40.

5. Ibid., pp. 41–72.

6. The campaign to "Let a Hundred Flowers Bloom, Diverse Schools of Thought Contend" [Bai hua qi fang, bai jia zheng ming] commenced on May 2, 1956. Its stated goal was to emphasize freedom of expression. It has also been suggested that the campaign was a facade to uncover dissidents and punish them through thought reform in the Anti-Rightist Campaign. On the Hundred Flowers Movement see *Ban Yue Kan* No. 13 (1956):74. An excellent review may be found in Roderick MacFarquhar, ed., *The Hundred Flowers Cam-*

paign and the Chinese Intellectuals (New York: Praeger Press, 1960). Also see Maurice Meisner, *Mao's China: A History of the People's Republic* (New York: Free Press, 1977) pp. 167–203. The Anti-Rightist Campaign was instituted on April 27, 1957. See *RMRB*, May 1 and 17, 1957; Goldman, *Literary Dissent*, pp. 158–202; Meisner, *Mao's China*, pp. 192–200. On the Anti-Japanese War period refer to Mao, "Talks at the Yenan Forum on Literature and Art," *SW*, 3:69–98.

7. Deng Xiaoping, who initially favored some liberalization, commented that more caution must be exercised in the publication of literature. He said that China's modernization demanded controls on dissent. *Zheng Ming* No. 29 (March 1980):11–23; *Wen Yi Bao* 11/12 (December 1979):8–26; *RMRB*, July 31, 1979. He reemphasized that point with the removal of Hu Yaobang from his post as Party General Secretary in 1987.

8. *RMRB*, November 13, 1979; *Shanghai Wenxue* 3 (March 1979):49–57.

9. In 1979, the Fourth Congress of Writers and Artists debated the subject. It was also the focus of the "Forum on Mao Zedong's Thinking with Regard to Literature and Art," May 6–12, 1982. FBIS-CHI-82-099, May 21, 1982, pp. K6–K10.

10. CCP, *Resolution on CPC History*, pp. 64–65.

11. Mao paraphrases Thesis XI from Marx's "Theses on Feuerbach" in Marx and Engels, *Selected Works*, 1:15.

12. Mao, "On New Democracy," *SW*, 2:340. Also see Mao, "Talks at the Yenan Forum on Literature and Art," *SW*, 3:86.

13. Ibid., 3:69–74, 78.

14. Anatoly Lunacharsky, "Theses on the Problems of Marxist Literary Criticism," in *On Literature and Art*, A. Lebedev, comp. (Moscow: Progress Publishers, 1973), p. 11.

15. Leon Trotsky, *Literature and Revolution* (Ann Arbor: University of Michigan Press, 1960), pp. 12–14, 193, 202.

16. Mao, *SW*, 3:70.

17. Ibid., 3:75.

18. Lunacharsky, "Problems of Literary Criticism," p. 13.

19. Mao, *SW*, 3:81.

20. Ibid., 3:82.

21. FBIS-CHI-82-099, May 21, 1982, pp. K6–K10.

22. *Monterey Peninsula Herald* (California), May 24, 1982.

23. *HQ* 21 (November 1, 1985):9–15.

24. His 1980 speech is translated in *Issues and Studies* (February 1982):67–106.

25. By adopting this perspective critical authors are often labeled as "bourgeois" or "counterrevolutionary" by the Party. For a survey of this literature see Richard King, " 'Wounds' and 'Exposure': Chinese Literature after the

Gang of Four,'' *Pacific Affairs* 54 (Spring 1981):82–99; Kai-yu Hsu, ed., *Literature of the People's Republic of China* (Bloomington: Indiana University Press, 1980), pp. 849–948; ''Revolutionary Literature in China,'' *Bulletin of Concerned Asian Scholars* 8, nos. 1-2 (White Plains, N.Y.: M. E. Sharpe, 1976); Jeffrey C. Kinkley, ed. *After Mao: Chinese Literature and Society* (Cambridge: Harvard University Press, 1985).

26. This assessment is also shared by King, ''Wounds and Exposure,'' pp. 82–83.

27. See the discussion of the function of literature in Du Shuying and Li Zhongyue, ''Dangxing yuanze yu yishu guilu'' [Party Principles and Artistic Laws], *WXPL* (May 1981):76–79; Zhang Chao, ''Yishu shilun'' [Truthfulness in Art], *WXPL* (June 1981):3–17.

28. King, ''Wounds and Exposure,'' p. 85, explains the derivation of this term. Also see *Chongfang de xianhua* [Fresh Flowers Bloom Again] (Shanghai: Wenyi chubanshe, 1979); Lee Yee, ed., *The New Realism: Writings from China after the Cultural Revolution* (New York: Hippocrene Books, 1983). On the Socialist Democracy Movement see ''The Rise and Decline of China's Democracy Movement,'' *Issues and Studies* 27 (January 1986):155–189.

29. I am indebted to Mr. Lau Yee-fui of the Universities Service Center, Hong Kong, and Mr. Ewald Cheer of the Defense Language Institute, Monterey, California, for their suggestions with regard to the use and interpretation of this literature.

30. Goldman, *Literary Dissent*, pp. 106–115. Also Yang I-fan, *The Case Against Hu Feng* (Hong Kong: Union Research Institute, 1976).

31. *China News Analysis* 89 (June 24, 1955):1–7.

32. Mao, *SW*, 3:70.

33. Hu Feng, quoted in Yang, *The Case against Hu Feng*, p. 20.

34. Goldman, *Literary Dissent*, pp. 7–9.

35. Ibid., p. 8.

36. Mao, *SW*, 3:73–74.

37. Ibid., p. 74.

38. Wang Meng, ''A New Young Man Arrives at the Organization Department,'' *Current Background*, no. 459 (Hong Kong: American Consulate, June 28, 1957), pp. 1–32; *RMWX* 9 (September 1956):29–43.

39. See notes 1 and 6. The slogan meant ''freedom of independent thinking, of debate, of creative work; freedom to criticize and freedom to express, maintain and reserve one's opinions of art, literature, or scientific research.'' *RMRB*, June 13, 1956.

40. *RMRB*, April 16, 1957.

41. Goldman, *Literary Dissent in China*, p. 180.

42. Ibid.

43. Ibid., pp. 203–242; *RMRB*, June 9, 1957; Goldman, ''The Unique

Blooming and Contending of 1961–62,'' *The China Quarterly* 37 (January-March 1969):54–83.

44. W. J. F. Jenner, ''1979: A New Start for Literature in China,'' *The China Quarterly* 86 (June 1981):282–284.

45. Ru Zhijuan, ''Jianji cuole di gushi'' [The Story of a Montage of Errors], *RMWX* 2 (February 1979):65–76. Ye Jianying glosses over the Great Leap Forward in *Speech at the Meeting in Celebration of the 30th Anniversary*, pp. 20–22.

46. Bai Hua, ''Yi shu xinzha'' [A Bundle of Letters], *RMWX* 1 (January 1980):24–40. For a commentary on ''workstyle'' and ''consciousness'' see *RMRB*, October 19, 1983 and *Beijing Review*, no. 42 (October 17, 1983):I–XII.

47. Translations of some journals from the Socialist Democracy Movement are available in JPRS 73215 (April 12, 1979); 73421 (May 10, 1979); 73728 (June 20, 1979); 73756 (June 26, 1979); 73787 (June 29, 1979); 73987 (August 9, 1979); 74591 (November 16, 1979). Some of the more significant articles from the journals are reprinted in Chinese in *Minzhu zhonghua* [Democratic China] (Hong Kong: Xianggang zhongwen daxue, 1982).

48. On the movement and its suppression by the Party see Roger Garside, *Coming Alive: China after Mao* (New York: McGraw-Hill, 1981). In my opinion part of the reaction by the CCP was an effect of the interest of foreign correspondents and diplomats. Many of those arrested, like Fu Yuehua, were sent to prison because of their contacts with foreigners. I prefer to see the foreign researcher, journalist, or diplomat temper his or her interest in political events in China, or ''quest for truth,'' with the realization that such interests can drastically affect the lives of others. The punishment for such contacts by the Chinese government can be brutal. See, for example, Liu Qing, *Yuzhong shouji* [Prison Notebooks] (Hong Kong: Baixing chubanshe, 1981).

49. Deng Xiaoping, *Deng Xiaoping wenxuan* [Selected Works] (Beijing: Renmin chubanshe, 1983), pp. 182–183.

50. *HQ* 21 (November 1, 1985):14–15.

51. *GMRB*, May 22, 1982.

52. King, ''Wounds and Exposure,'' pp. 85–86; Lu Xinhua and Liu Xinwu, eds., *The Wounded: New Stories of the Cultural Revolution*, trans. Geremie Barme and Bennett Lee (Hong Kong: Joint Publishing Co., 1979).

53. See Wen Hua, ''Dangqian wenyi chuangzuo xuyao zhuyi de jige wenti'' [Several Questions which Call for Attention in Literature and Art Creation at Present], *HQ* (November 7, 1982):29–31.

54. On interpretive understanding see Clifford Geertz, ''Deep Play: Notes on the Balinese Cockfight,'' in *Interpretive Social Science: A Reader*, ed. Paul Rabinow and William Sullivan (Berkeley: University of California Press, 1979),

pp. 181–223; Geertz, *Negara: A Theater State in 19th Century Bali* (Princeton: Princeton University Press, 1980); Paul Ricoeur, *The Conflict of Interpretations: Essays in Hermeneutics* (Evanston: Northwestern University Press, 1974); Ricoeur, *Freud and Philosophy*.

55. Zhou Yongnian, "Zhuren" [Master], *RMWX* 3 (March 1976):32–41.

56. Liu Binyan, "Between Human and Demon," in *The New Realism: Writings from China after the Cultural Revolution*, ed. Lee Yee (New York: Hippocrene Books, 1983), pp. 195–243. Liu was involved in the late 1986–early 1987 Party upheaval that led to the dismissal of Hu Yaobang as Party Secretary General.

57. Ibid., p. 195.

58. Xu Huaizhong, "Xixian yishi" [An Anecdote from the Western Front], *RMWX* 1 (January 1980):3–23.

59. Ibid., pp. 8–10.

60. Jiang Zilong, "Tie xian zhuan" [Commentary on a Shovel], *RMWX* 4 (April 1976):39–55.

61. The policy directives may be reviewed in *RMRB*, October 13, 1957 and December 31, 1964.

62. "Bourgeois right" is the necessary and continued presence in socialist society of inequities that were inherited from, and are institutional to, the capitalist system. Examples are the commodity system of exchange and the use of currency as a medium of exchange; see *HQ* 11 (June 1, 1985):12–17.

63. This same point was made by Ye Wenling, "Nianfan" [A New Year's Meal], *RMWX* 11 (November 1977):55–62.

64. Jiang Zilong, "Jidian juzhang de yi tian" [A Day in the Life of the Electrical Equipment Bureau Chief], *RMWX* 1 (January 1976):45–61.

65. Ibid., p. 50.

66. Jiang Zilong, "Yige gongchang mishu de riji" [A Factory Secretary's Diary], in *RMWX*, ed., *1980 Nian quan guo youxiu duanpian xiaoshuo pingxuan* [The 1980 Critical Collection of the Entire Nation's Outstanding Short Stories] (Shanghai: Shanghai wenyi chubanshe, 1981), pp. 170–195. Note that this is *mishu*, a clerk or personal assistant, not *shuji*, a secretary (leader) of a committee or Party organ.

67. Qin Yanshen, " 'Tiao' duizhang jishi," *RMWX* 1 (January 1978):82–86. *Tiao* means stupid or muddleheaded in the Hunan dialect.

68. Liu Wu, "Tongzhi" [Comrade], *RMWX* 2 (February 1978):85–89.

69. Fox Butterfield, *China: Alive in the Bitter Sea* (London: Hodder and Stoughton, 1982), passim. For more on the problem see Roger Garside, *Coming Alive*.

70. Jiao Zuyao, "Zhao huan," *RMWX* 7 (July 1980):81–86.

71. While in China I ran into several situations where this was the case.

The most glaring incident involved the daughter of a court official who allegedly maintained a separate residence, procured with the assistance of her parent, where she could meet with a foreign lover.

72. Li Zhun, "Da nian chuyi," pp. 62–68.

73. See *Han-Ying Cidian* (Beijing: Beijing Institute of Foreign Languages, 1979), p. 976.

74. CCP, *Resolution on CPC History*.

75. These points were consistently made by Zhou Yang, chairman of the China Federation of Literary and Art Circles, *RMRB*, March 16, 1983.

76. A similar tendency in the USSR is described in Hedrick Smith, *The Russians* (New York: Quadrangle Press, 1976). On alienation see Karl Marx, *Economic and Philosophical Manuscripts*, in *Early Writings*, Rodney Livingstone, trans. (New York: Vintage Books, 1975), pp. 322–335, 383–395; Donald J. Munro, "The Chinese View of 'Alienation,' " *The China Quarterly* 59 (July-September 1974):580–582.

77. Mao, *SW*, 2:56–57.

78. The Constitution of the Communist Party of China, Article 10 (1).

79. Stanislaw Ossowski, *Class Structure in the Social Consciousness* (New York: Free.Press, 1963), pp. 104–105.

80. Zygmunt Bauman, Officialdom and Class: Bases of Inequality in Socialist Society, in *The Social Analysis of Class Structure*, ed. Frank Parkin (London: Tavistock Publishers, 1974), pp. 134–139.

81. The classic study of how the Party operates is Franz Schurmann, *Ideology and Organization in Communist China*.

82. Constitution of the CCP, Article 8.

83. Ibid., Article 30.

CHAPTER 5

1. See chapter 4.

2. Li Yizhe, "Guanyu shehui zhuyi de minzhu yu fazhi [On the Socialist Democracy and Legal System]," in *Minzhu Zhonghua* (Hong Kong: Zhongwen daxue, 1983), p. 55. Li Yizhe is a pen name taken from the surname and given names of three of the authors of the "manifesto": Li Zhengtian, Chen Yiyang, and Wang Xizhe. The fourth author was Guo Hongzhi. In 1977 they were all arrested and imprisoned but were released and rehabilitated in 1978. Wang was arrested again three years later. For biographies of Chinese dissidents see *Qishi niandai* 6 (June 1981):16–17.

3. Li Yizhe, "Guanyu shehui zhuyi," p. 56.

4. *The Washington Post*, July 29, 1983.

5. Socialist Democracy Movement is a coalition of Chinese who published underground literature critical of the CCP and who sought political self-deter-

mination free of Party dominance. A collection of the literature in its original form may be found at the Universities Service Center, Hong Kong. Some of the publications call for a reconsideration of Marxism, questioning its validity in practice. These include *Tansuo*, *Minzhuqiang*, *Renmin luntan*, *Zhongguo renquan*, and *Qimeng*. Other publications, such as *Beijing zhichun* and *Siwu luntan*, seek to revive principles of Chinese communism under constitutional legal guarantees. For reprints in Chinese see Claude Widor, ed., *Documents sur le mouvement democratique chinois: 1978–1980*, vol. 1 (Paris: Editions de l'École des hautes études en sciences sociales, 1981); and Institute for the Study of Chinese Communist Problems, ed., *Collection of the Underground Mainland Publications*, 11 vols. (Taipei: Shanghai Press, 1981). I am grateful to the curators of the East Asian Collection, Hoover Institution on War, Revolution and Peace, for their assistance and permission to review certain original manuscripts from the movement, as well as the staff of the Universities Service Center, Hong Kong, for granting me access to their materials.

6. Wright, *Class, Crisis and the State*, p. 41.

7. Production for a market occurs in both capitalist and socialist states. The reader should understand market such that goods or services are produced and offered for consumption through the exchange of commodities or money. Demand in a planned economy does not necessarily affect price.

8. Jaroslav Krejci, *Social Change and Stratification in Postwar Czechoslovakia*, p. 129.

9. Wright, *Class, Crisis and the State*, p. 41; idem, "Class and Occupation," *Theory and Society* 9 (January 1980):177–214.

10. Idem, *Class, Crisis and the State*, p. 41.

11. See Carl Beck, "Patterns and Problems of Governance," in C. Mesa-Logo and C. Beck, eds. *Comparative Socialist Systems* (Pittsburgh: University of Pennsylvania Press, 1975), p. 128; Andrei Amalrik, *Will the Soviet Union Survive until 1984?* (New York: Harper & Row, 1970), p. 17; Leslie Benson, "Market Socialism and Class Structure," in Frank Parkin, *The Social Analysis of Class Structure* (London: Tavistock Publishers, 1974), pp. 257–260.

12. See Jan S. Prybyla, *The Chinese Economy: Problems and Policies*, 2d ed. (Columbia: University of South Carolina Press, 1981); Rosalie L. Tung, *Chinese Industrial Society after Mao* (Toronto: D. C. Heath, 1982); Alexander Eckstein, *China's Economic Revolution* (New York: Cambridge University Press, 1977); Barry Richman, *Industrial Society in Communist China* (New York: Random House, 1969); Lin Wei and Arnold V. Chao, eds., *China's Economic Reforms* (Philadelphia: University of Pennsylvania Press, 1982).

13. Thomas G. Rawski, *China's Transition to Industrialism* (Ann Arbor: University of Michigan Press, 1980), pp. 110–114; Jan S. Prybyla, *Issues in Socialist Economic Modernization* (New York: Praeger Publishers, 1980), pp. 3–5, 39–69.

14. Prybyla, *Socialist Economic Modernization*, p. 4.

15. Eckstein, *China's Economic Revolution*, chap. 8.

16. Prybyla, ''Key Issues in the Chinese Economy,'' *Asian Survey* 21 (September 1981):932. For a general outline of China's five-year plans see Leo A. Orleans, ''Soviet Perceptions of China's Economic Development,'' in *Chinese Economy Post-Mao*, U.S. Congress, Joint Economic Committee Print, 95th Congress, 2d Session (Washington, D.C.: Government Printing Office, 1978), pp. 126–139.

17. Xue Muqiao, *Current Economic Problems in China*, trans. and ed. K. K. Fung (Boulder: Westview Press, 1982), p. xiii.

18. Bruce L. Reynolds, ''Reform in Industrial Management: An Empirical Report,'' in *China under the Four Modernizations*, Part 1, U.S. Congress, Joint Economic Committee Print, 97th Congress, 2d Session (Washington, D.C.: Government Printing Office, 1982), p. 123.

19. Ibid., p. 134.

20. Xue, *Current Economic Problems*, pp. 135–136; Sun Yuefang, *Shehui zhuyi jingji de ruogan lilun wenti*, pp. 57–79.

21. Xue, *Current Economic Problems*, p. 59.

22. Albert S. Peterson, ''China: Transportation Developments, 1971–1980,'' in *China under the Four Modernizations*, pp. 148–150.

23. Ibid., p. 140.

24. Ibid., p. 139.

25. Xue, *Current Economic Problems*, p. 58.

26. *1982 Zhongguo jingji nianjian* [Almanac of China's Economy] (Beijing: Jingji guanli zazhishe, 1982), p. II-3.

27. Ibid., II-16–II-18.

28. Trip notes: Visit to the Lanzhou Chemical Industries Corporation, Gansu Province, May 18–19, 1983.

29. Xue, *Current Economic Problems*, p. 138.

30. Rawski, *China's Transition to Industrialism*, p. 113.

31. Xiao Liang, ''Changing the Leadership System in State Enterprises,'' in Wei and Chao, *China's Economic Reforms*, p. 151.

32. Gong Min, ''Letter to President Carter,'' *Qimeng* 3 (January 1, 1979) in JPRS 73215 (April 12, 1979):51.

33. JPRS 73421 (May 10, 1979):3.

34. Ibid.

35. Ibid., p. 15.

36. Ibid., p. 17.

37. Ibid.

38. Wei Jingshen (published under the pseudonym Jin Sheng), ''Di wuge xiandaihua—minzhu yu chita'' [The Fifth Modernization—Democracy, etc.], in *Minzhu Zhonghua*, p. 170.

39. Ibid., p. 172.

40. Ibid., p. 189.

41. JPRS 73787 (June 29, 1979):45.

42. JPRS 73987 (August 9, 1979):15.

43. JPRS 73728 (June 20, 1979):35.

44. *Wen Hui Bao* (Shanghai), September 8, 1979. Translated in FBIS-CHI (October 24, 1979):L14-L19.

45. JPRS 73728 (June 20, 1979):59.

46. See Monte Ray Bullard and Edward C. O'Dowd, "Defining the role of the PLA in the Post-Mao Era," *Asian Survey* 26 (June 1986):706–720.

47. JPRS 73728 (June 20, 1979):59.

48. Robert Delfs, FEER, January 29, 1982, pp. 10–12; FEER, February 5, 1982, p. 13. Also see Deng Xiaoping, *Deng Xiaoping tongzhi tanduan zhengdangfeng wenti* [Comrade Deng Xiaoping Discusses Questions with Regard to Proper Party Rectification] (Jiangsu: Hongqi chubanshe, 1981); idem, "Persist in the Party Line, Improve Work Methods," in *Selected Works of Deng Xiaoping*, pp. 259–266.

49. FBIS-CHI-82-053 (March 18, 1982):Q6–Q7.

50. *RMRB*; April 4, 1982.

51. *Guanyu dangnei zhengzhi shenghuo de ruogan zhunze* [On the Guiding Principles for Inner-Party Political Life] (Beijing: Renmin chubanshe, 1980); Liu Shaoqi, "How to Be a Good Communist," in *Three Essays on Party-Building* (Beijing: Foreign Languages Press, 1980), pp. 1–98.

52. Peasants may own their own homes in the countryside. In some cases the residents of cities may own homes; for instance, in Nanjing I was invited to the home of a Party cadre which was once located on farm land. However, as the city grew the house was incorporated into the urban area.

53. FBIS-CHI-82-017 (January 26, 1982):K5–K7.

54. FBIS-CHI-82-019 (January 28, 1982):K1.

55. FBIS-CHI-82-031 (February 16, 1982):K16.

56. *HQ* 3 (February 1, 1982):44–45.

57. FBIS-CHI-82-052 (March 17, 1982):R2–R3.

58. Ibid., R3.

59. FBIS-CHI-82-954 (March 19, 1982):O1–O2.

60. FBIS-CHI-82-055 (March 22, 1982):K11.

61. FBIS-CHI-82-066 (April 6, 1982):W2.

62. FBIS-CHI-82-192 (October 4, 1982):W3.

63. Ibid.

64. FBIS-CHI-82-072 (April 14, 1982):Q1–Q2.

65. FBIS-CHI-82-056 (March 23, 1982):Q1–Q6.

66. FBIS-CHI-82-060 (March 29, 1982):Q2.

67. FBIS-CHI-82-071 (April 13, 1982):W2.

68. FBIS-CHI-82-066 (April 6, 1982):W2–W3.

69. FBIS-CHI-82-083 (April 29, 1982):P1–P2. On the bonus system in effect see Larry M. Wortzel, ''Incentive Mechanisms and Remuneration in China: Policies of the Eleventh Central Committee,'' *Asian Survey* 21 (September 1981):972–974.

70. *RMRB*, November 25, 1982.

71. FBIS-CHI-82-101 (May 25, 1982):S3–S4.

72. FBIS-CHI-82-200 (October 15, 1982):K7.

73. *RMRB*, January 4, 1980.

74. Lin Boye and Shen Zhe, ''Ping suowei fandui guanliao zhuyi zhe jieji'' [Commenting on the So-Called Opposition to the Class of Bureaucrats], *HQ* 5 (March 1981):12–18. A similar argument may be found in an article entitled ''Does a 'Bureaucratic Class' Exist within the Party,'' in *Zhongguo qingnian bao*, which was translated in the FBIS daily report of February 23, 1981, pp. L27–L30.

75. Lin and Shen, ''Ping suowei fandui guanliao zhuyi,'' pp. 14–15.

76. Ibid.

77. Ibid., pp. 16–17. Also see FBIS-CHI-82-197, pp. K1–K7; JPRS 76989 (December 18, 1981):34–36.

78. FBIS-CHI-82-161 (August 26, 1982):T1.

79. Ibid.

80. *RMRB*, March 30, 1982.

81. *New York Times*, March 28, 1985.

82. Ibid.

83. Lin and Shen, ''Ping suowei fandui guanliao zhuyi,'' pp. 12–14.

84. Ibid., p. 14.

85. Ibid., pp. 13–14.

CHAPTER 6

1. Jingji yanjiu bianjibu, *Shehui zhuyi zhengzhi jingjixue ruogan jiben lilun wenti* [Certain Theoretical Questions on Socialist Political Economy] (Jinan: Shandong chubanshe, 1980), pp. 17–36.

2. Review the discussion in chapter 5.

3. Mihailo Markovic, ''Socialism and Self-Management,'' in *Self-Governing Socialism*, vol. 1, Branko Horvat et al., ed. (White Plains, N.Y.: International Arts and Sciences Press, 1975), pp. 416–417; also see Najdan Pasic, ''The Idea of Direct Self-Managing Democracy and Socialization of Policy-Making,'' in ibid., pp. 34–35.

4. Pasic, ''The Idea of Direct Self-Managing Democracy,'' p. 35.

5. Kostas Axelos, *Alienation, Praxis, and Techne in the Thought of Karl Marx*, pp. 215–219.

6. Karl Marx, "Economic and Philosophical Manuscripts (1844)," in *Early Writings*, Rodney Livingstone, trans. (New York: Vintage Books, 1975), p. 287.
7. Ibid., p. 348.
8. Ibid., p. 324.
9. Ibid., p. 348.
10. *Beijing zhi qun* [Beijing Spring] 2 (January 27, 1979):1–2. Also see Branco Horvat et al., *Self-Governing Socialism*, 2:34–150.
11. Markovic, "Socialism and Self-Management," p. 417.
12. Marx and Engels, "Feuerbach," p. 34.
13. Ibid., pp. 34–35.
14. Xue Muqiao, *China's Socialist Economy* (Beijing: Foreign Languages Press, 1981), p. 204; Sun Shangqing et al., "Duiyu woguo jingji jiegou wenti de chubu yanjiu" [Tentative Research on Problems of China's Economic Structure], in *Shehui zhuyi zhengzhi jingjixue ruogan jiben lilun wenti* (Jinan: Shandong Chubanshe, 1980), pp. 17–36.
15. *Beijing zhi qun* 2, p. 2.
16. See the discussion of the economic infrastructure in chapter 5.
17. Markovic, "Socialism and Self-Management," p. 417.
18. The CCP, as the vanguard of the working class, exercises a dictatorship over the elements of society judged to be enemies of the Party program. See Mao Zedong, "On the People's Democratic Dictatorship," *SW*, 4:411–424.
19. Markovic, "Socialism and Self-Management," p. 417.
20. *RMRB*, April 9, 1982; also see *RMRB*, April 15, 1982.
21. Ibid., April 15, 1982.
22. Ibid., April 9, 1982.
23. Notwithstanding the argument by Georg Konrad and Ivan Szelenyi that intellectuals are emerging as a class that rules by virtue of its authority to control all aspects of a society. See Konrad and Szelenyi, *Intellectuals on the Road to Class Power* (New York: Harcourt Brace Jovanovich, 1979). Also see Alvin W. Gouldner, *The Future of Intellectuals and the Rise of the New Class* (New York: Seabury Press, 1979). If intellectuals were to form a class solely through their ability to control society, that would be parallel to the role of the Party. In either case the concept of class becomes so radically changed that it loses its meaning in the Marxian sense and returns to its traditional meaning of an identifiable social grouping.
24. Frederick Engels, "Letter to Otto Boenigk: August 21, 1890," in *Selected Works*, 3:486.
25. V. I. Lenin, "What Is to Be Done? Burning Questions of Our Movement," in *Collected Works* (Moscow: Progress Publishers, 1964), 5:375–376.
26. *Resolution on CPC History*, p. 80.
27. Ibid., pp. 80–81.

28. John P. Burns, "The Election of Production Team Cadres in Rural China: 1958–1974," *China Quarterly* 74 (June 1978):294–295.

29. Ibid., p. 295.

30. Ibid.

31. Ibid., pp. 294–296.

32. O. I. Shkaratan, "Social Groups in the Working Class of a Developed Socialist Society," in *Social Stratification and Mobility in the USSR*, Murray Yanowitch and Wesley A. Fisher, trans. and ed. (White Plains, N.Y.: International Arts and Sciences Press, 1973), p. 83.

33. Ibid.

34. Jingji yanjiu bianjibu, *Shehui zhuyi zhengzhi jingjixue*, pp. 1–16, 18–21.

35. Howard Sherman, *Radical Political Economy* (New York: Basic Books, 1972), p. 38; Thomas Sowell, *Marxism* (New York: William Morrow, 1985), pp. 89, 113. Note that Sowell does not recognize a "theory of value," only a "concept of value."

36. Sherman, *Radical Political Economy*, p. 40.

37. Wortzel, "Incentive Mechanisms and Remuneration in China," p. 967; Alexander Eckstein, *China's Economic Revolution* (New York: Cambridge University Press, 1977), p. 300.

38. Prybyla, *The Chinese Economy*, p. 157.

39. Ibid.

40. Ibid.

41. *BR* 21 (May 21, 1984):9.

42. *BR* 20 (May 16, 1982):7.

43. Ibid.

44. Author's trip notes, May 1983.

45. *Time*, April 30, 1984, pp. 26–30.

46. *Zhongguo jingji nianjian 1982* (Beijing: Jingji guanli zazhishe, 1982), pp. V1–V92; Tang Tsou et al., "The Responsibility System in Agriculture," pp. 41–103.

47. Wortzel, "Incentive Mechanisms and Remuneration in China," p. 971.

48. Dale Bratton, "University Admissions Policies in China, 1970–1978," *Asian Survey* 19 (October 1979):1008–1022; Suzanne Pepper, *China's Universities* (Ann Arbor: University of Michigan Press, 1984), pp. 114–116.

49. Suzanne Pepper, "Education and Revolution: The 'Chinese Model' Revisited," *Asian Survey* 18 (September 1978):886–888; idem, *China's Universities*, pp. 50–54, 114–116.

50. Pepper, *China's Universities*, pp. 21–22, 30.

51. Ibid., pp. 21–24.

52. See C. H. Chai, "Changes in Property Rights and Income Distribution under China's Baogan Daohu System," paper presented at the Conference on

Development and Distribution in China, Centre for Asian Studies, Hong Kong University, March 1983. Also see the discussion by Tsou et al., which explains the policies while acting as apologist for Dazhai and the admission by the CCP Central Committee that much of the economic data were falsified. Tsou et al., "The Responsibility System in Agriculture," pp. 41–103. The authors politely avoid the use of the word "falsify" and instead refer to the "establishment and maintenance of [economic] models through artificial and deceptive methods."

53. "A Review of Current Agricultural Policies in China," Economic Section, American Consulate General, Hong Kong (October 14, 1980).

54. This, of course, further assumed that class was a viable way to understand the articulation of sociopolitical interest in England in the mid-nineteenth century.

55. Milovan Djilas, *The New Class* (Holt, Rinehart & Winston, 1957).

56. See the discussion of "partynomial authority" in Zygmunt Bauman, "Officialdom and Class, Bases of Inequality in Socialist Society," in Frank Parkin, ed. *The Social Analysis of Class Structure* (London: Tavistock Publishers, 1974), pp. 134–136.

Bibliography

GENERAL REFERENCES

"A Review of Current Agricultural Policies in China." Economic Section, American Consulate General, Hong Kong. October 14, 1982.

Almond, Gabriel. *The Politics of Developing Areas*. Princeton: Princeton University Press, 1960.

Althusser, Louis. *For Marx*. London: New Left Books, 1977.

Althusser, Louis, and Etienne Balibar. *Reading Capital*. London: New Left Books, 1970.

Amalrek, Andrei. *Will the Soviet Union Survive until 1984?* New York: Harper & Row, 1970.

Anderson, Charles H. *The Political Economy of Social Class*. Englewood Cliffs, N.J.: Prentice-Hall, 1974.

Atkinson, A. B. *The Economics of Inequality*. Oxford: Clarendon Press, 1976.

Avineri, Shlomo. *The Social and Political Thought of Karl Marx*. New York: Cambridge University Press, 1968.

Axelos, Kostas. *Alienation, Praxis, and Techne in the Thought of Karl Marx*. Translated by Ronald Bruzina. Austin: University of Texas Press, 1976.

Axilrod, Eric. *The Political Economy of the Chinese Revolution*. Hong Kong: Union Research Institute, 1972.

Backstrom, Charles H., and Gerald D. Hursh. *Survey Research*. Evanston: Northwestern University Press, 1963.

Bahro, Rudolf. *The Alternative in Eastern Europe*. Manchester, U.K.: New Left Books, 1978.

Bai Hua. *Unrequited Love*. JPRS-79676. China Report No. 248. Washington, D.C.: Government Printing Office, December 16, 1981.

Balazs, Etienne. *Chinese Civilization and Bureaucracy*. New Haven: Yale University Press, 1964.

Barnett, A. Doak. *Cadres Bureaucracy and Political Power in China*. New York: Columbia University Press, 1967.

Baum, Richard. "Science and Culture in Contemporary China: The Roots of Retarded Modernization." *Asian Survey* 22 (December 1982):1166–1186.

Bauman, Zygmunt. *Hermeneutics and Social Science: Approaches to Understanding*. London: Hutchinson, 1978.

———. "Officialdom and Class: Bases of Inequality in Socialist Society." In *The Social Analysis of Class Structure*, ed. Frank Parkin, 129–148. London: Tavistock Publishers, 1974.

Beck, Carl. "Patterns and Problems of Governance." In *Comparative Socialist Systems*, ed. C. Mesa-Lago and C. Beck, 123–146. Pittsburgh: University of Pittsburgh Press, 1975.

Benson, Leslie. "Market Socialism and Class Structure: Manual Workers and Management Power in the Yugoslav Enterprise." In *The Social Analysis of Class Power*, ed. Frank Parkin, 257–268. London: Tavistock Publishers, 1974.

Berger, Peter L. and Thomas Luckman. *The Social Construction of Reality*. New York: Doubleday, 1966.

Bettelheim, Charles. *Cultural Revolution and Industrial Organization in China*. Cambridge: Cambridge University Press, 1973.

Bettelheim, Charles, and Neil G. Burton. *China since Mao*. New York: Monthly Review Press, 1978.

Bratton, Dale. "University Admissions Policies in China, 1970–1978." *Asian Survey* 19 (October 1979): 1008–1022.

Brodsgaard, Kjeld Eric. "The Democracy Movement in China, 1978–1979: Opposition Movements, Wall Poster Campaigns, and Underground Journals." *Asian Survey* 7 (July 1981): 747–774.

Bromke, Adam. "Poland: The Cliff's Edge." *Foreign Policy* 41 (Winter 1980–1981):154–162.

Brown, Archie, and Jack Gray, eds. *Political Culture and Political Change in Communist States*, 2d ed. New York: Holmes and Meier, 1979.

Brugger, William S. *Democracy and Organization in the Chinese Industrial Enterprise*. New York: Cambridge University Press, 1976.

Brus, Wlodzmierz. *The Economics and Politics of Socialism*. London: Routledge & Kegan Paul, 1975.

———. *Socialist Ownership and Political Systems*. London: Routledge & Kegan Paul, 1975.

Bullard, Monte Ray. "People's Republic of China Elite Studies: A Review of the Literature." *Asian Survey* 19 (August 1979):789–800.

Bullard, Monte Ray and Edward C. O'Dowd. "Defining the Role of the PLA in the Post-Mao Era." *Asian Survey* 26 (June 1986):706–720.

Burns, John P. "The Election of Production Team Cadres in Rural China: 1958–1974." *China Quarterly* 74 (June 1978):273–296.

———. "Rural Guangdong's 'Second Economy' 1962–1974." *China Quarterly* 88 (December 1981):629–644.

Butterfield, Fox. *China: Alive in the Bitter Sea*. London: Hodder and Stoughton, 1982.

Castoriades, Cornelius. "Socialism and Autonomous Society." *Telos* 43 (Spring 1980):91–106.

Chai, C. H. "Changes in Property Rights and Income Distribution under China's Baogan Daohu System." Paper presented at the Conference on Development and Distribution in China, Centre of Asian Studies, University of Hong Kong, March 14–17, 1983.

Chan, Anita, Stanley Rosen, and Johnathan Unger. "Students and Class Warfare: The Social Roots of the Red Guard Conflict in Guangzhou." *China Quarterly* 83 (September 1980):379–446.

Chan, Chung-li. *The Chinese Gentry*. Seattle: University of Washington Press, 1955.

Chan, Parris H. "Chinese Politics: Deng's Turbulent Quest." *Problems of Communism* 30 (January-February 1981):12–31.

Chang Ch'un-Ch'iao. *On Exercising All-Round Dictatorship over the Bourgeoisie*. Beijing: Foreign Languages Press, 1975.

Chen Ting-chung. "The Pay Raise Program in Mainland China." *Issues and Studies* 2 (February 1978):1–11.

Chen Yun and Hu Yaobang. "On Party Discipline." *Beijing Review* 51 (December 22, 1980):4.

Cheng, Chu-yuan. *China's Economic Development: Growth and Structural Change*. Boulder, Co.: Westview Press, 1982.

Cheng, J. Chester, trans. *Documents of Dissent: Chinese Political Thought since Mao*. Stanford: Hoover Institution Press, 1980.

Chi Hsin. *Teng Hsiao-ping: A Political Biography*. Hong Kong: Cosmos Books, 1978.

Chinese Communist Party. *Resolution on CPC History (1949–1981)*. Beijing: Foreign Languages Press, 1981.

Chow Tse-tsung. *The May Fourth Movement: Intellectual Revolution in Modern China*. Cambridge: Harvard University Press, 1960.

Christie, Anthony. *Chinese Mythology*. Middlesex, U.K.: Hamlyn Publishing Group, 1968.

Ch'u, T'ung-tsu. "Chinese Class Structure and Its Ideology." In *Chinese Thought and Institutions*, ed. John K. Fairbank, 235–250. Chicago: University of Chicago Press, 1957.

———. *Han Social Structure*, ed. Jack L. Dull. Seattle: University of Washington Press, 1972.

Clarkson, Stephen. *The Soviet Theory of Development*. Toronto: University of Toronto Press, 1978.

Cocks, Paul. "Bureaucracy and Party Control." In *Comparative Socialist Systems*, ed. Carl Beck and C. Mesa-Lagos, 215–248. Pittsburgh: University of Pittsburgh Press, 1975.

Confucius. *The Analects* (Lun yu), trans. James Legge. New York: Dover Publications, 1971.

Connerton, Paul. *Critical Sociology: Selected Readings*. New York: Penguin Books, 1976.

Creel, H. G. *Chinese Thought from Confucius to Mao Tse-tung*. Chicago: University of Chicago Press, 1953.

———. "The Beginnings of Bureaucracy in China: The Origin of the Hsien" *Journal of Asian Studies* 23 (February 1964):155–184.

Crompton, Rosemary and John Buggay. *Economy and Class Structure*. New York: St. Martin's Press, 1978.

Cuthbertson, Gilbert Morris. *Political Myth and Epic*. Ann Arbor: Michigan State University Press, 1957.

Dahrendorf, Rolf. *Class and Class Conflict in Industrial Society*. Stanford: Stanford University Press, 1959.

———. *Conflict after Class: New Perspectives on the Theory of Social and Political Conflict*. London: Longmans, Green, 1967.

Dallmayr, Fred R. and Thomas A. McCarthy, eds. *Understanding and Social Inquiry*. Notre Dame, Ind.: University of Notre Dame Press, 1977.

Decision of the Central Committee of the Chinese Communist Party Concerning the Great Proletarian Cultural Revolution. Beijing: Foreign Languages Press, 1966.

Delfs, Robert. "Intellectuals on Ice." *Far Eastern Economic Review* (February 9, 1984):32–33.

Deng Xiaoping. *Selected Works of Deng Xiaoping*. Beijing: Foreign Languages Press, 1984.

Dittmer, Lowell. *Liu Shao-ch'i and the Chinese Cultural Revolution*. Berkeley: University of California Press, 1974.

———. "Line Struggle in Theory and Practice: The Origins of the Cultural Revolution Reconsidered." *China Quarterly* 72 (December 1977):675–712.

———. "The Radical Critique of Political Interest, 1966–1978." *Modern China* 4 (October 1980):363–396.

Djilas, Milovan. *The New Class*. New York: Holt, Rinehart & Winston, 1957.

———. *The Unperfect Society: Beyond the New Class*. New York: Harcourt, Brace and World, 1969.

Donnithorne, Audrey. *China's Economic System*. London: Allen & Unwin, 1967.

Dunn, John. *Western Political Theory in the Face of the Future*. London: Cambridge University Press, 1979.

Durr, Heiner. "Regional Inequalities of Rural Income under the Influence of the Modernization Program." Paper presented at the Conference on Development and Distribution in China, Centre of Asian Studies, University of Hong Kong, March 14–17, 1983.

Eberhard, Wolfram. *Conquerors and Rulers: Social Forces in Medieval China*. Leiden: E. J. Brill, 1965.

———. *Folktales of China*. London: Routledge & Kegan Paul, 1965.

———. *Social Mobility in Traditional China*. 2d. Rev. Ed. Leiden: E. J. Brill, 1970.

Eckstein, Alexander. *China's Economic Revolution*. New York: Cambridge University Press, 1977.

Ehrenberg, John R. "Marxism and the Contradictions of the Proletarian State." Paper delivered at the American Political Science Association 1979 Annual Meeting, August 31–September 3, 1979.

Eisenstadt, S. N. *Revolution and the Transformation of Societies*. New York: Free Press, 1978.

Engels, Frederick. "Critique of the Gotha Programme." In Karl Marx and Frederick Engels, *Selected Works*, 3:9–10. Moscow: Progress Publishers, 1970.

———. "Letter to Otto Boenigk, August 21, 1980." In Karl Marx and Frederick Engels, *Selected Works*, 3:486. Moscow: Progress Publishers, 1970.

———. "The Origin of the Family, Private Property, and the State." In Karl Marx and Frederick Engels, *Selected Works*, 3:191–334. Moscow: Progress Publishers, 1970.

Fang Sheng. "The Revival of Individual Economy in Urban Areas." In *China's Economic Reforms*, ed. Lin Wei and Arnold Chao, 172–185. Philadelphia: University of Pennsylvania Press, 1982.

Feher, Ferenc and Agnes Heller. *Hungary, 1956 Revisited*. New York: Allen & Unwin, 1983.

Feher, Ferenc and Agnes Heller et al. *Dictatorship over Needs*. New York: St. Martin's Press, 1983.

Fei Hsiao-t'ung. *China's Gentry*. Chicago: University of Chicago Press, 1953.

Feuerwerker, Albert. "A White Horse May or May Not Be a Horse, but Megahistory Is Not Economic History." In *The Development of Underdevelopment in China*, ed. Philip C. C. Huang, 81–89. White Plains, N.Y.: M. E. Sharpe, 1980.

Filstead, William J., ed. *Qualitative Methodology: Firsthand Involvement with the Social World*. Chicago: Markham, 1970.

Fletcher, M. D. "Industrial Relations in China: The New Line." *Pacific Affairs* 1 (Spring 1979):78–94.

Foucault, Michel. *Madness and Civilization*. New York: Pantheon Books, 1965.

———. *The Order of Things: An Archaeology of the Human Sciences*. New York: Vintage Books, 1973.

———. *The Archaeology of Knowledge*. New York: Harper & Row, 1976.

Fried, Morton H. "Socioeconomic Relations in Pre-Communist China." *Modern China* 4 (October 1982):485–489.

Frolic, B. Michael. *Mao's People: Sixteen Portraits of Life in Revolutionary China*. Cambridge: Harvard University Press, 1980.

Fung Yu-lan. *A Short History of Chinese Philosophy*. New York: Free Press, 1948.

Gadamer, Hans-Georg. *Truth and Method*. New York: Seabury Press, 1975.

Galtung, Johan. *Theory and Methods of Social Research*. London: Allen & Unwin, 1967.

Garside, Roger. *Coming Alive: China after Mao*. New York: McGraw Hill, 1981.

Garson, David G. *Political Science Methods*. Boston: Holbrook Press, 1976.

Geertz, Clifford. "Deep Play: Notes on the Balinese Cockfight." In *Interpretive Social Science: A Reader*, ed. Paul Rubinow and William Sullivan, 181–223. Berkeley: University of California Press, 1979.

———. *Negara: A Theater State in 19th Century Bali*. Princeton: Princeton University Press, 1980.

Giddens, Anthony. *The Class Structure of Advanced Societies*. London: Hutchinson, 1973.

———. "Classes, Capitalism, and the State: A Review Essay." *Theory and Society* 96 (November 1980):878–894.

Goldman, Merle. "The Unique Blooming and Contending of 1961–62," *China Quarterly* 37 (January-March 1969):54–83.

———. *Literary Dissent in Communist China*. New York: Atheneum Press, 1971.

Gouldner, Alvin W. *The Future of Intellectuals and the Rise of the New Class*. New York: Seabury Press, 1979.

Granet, Marcel. *Chinese Civilization*. New York: Alfred A. Knopf, 1930.

Gray, Jack and Gordon White. *China's New Development Strategy*. New York: Academic Press, 1982.

Griffin, Keith and Kimberly Griffin. "Institutional Change and Income Distribution in the Chinese Countryside." Paper presented at the Conference on Development and Distribution in China, Centre of Asian Studies, University of Hong Kong, March 14–17, 1983.

Gurley, John G. *China's Economy and the Maoist Strategy*. New York: Monthly Review Press, 1976.

Habermas, Jürgen. *Knowledge and Human Interests*. Boston: Beacon Press, 1971.

———. *Theory and Practice*. Boston: Beacon Press, 1974.

Haeger, John Winthrop, ed. *Crisis and Prosperity in Sung China*. Tucson: University of Arizona Press, 1975.

Harding, Harry. *Organizing China: The Problem of Bureaucracy*. Stanford: Stanford University Press, 1981.

Hegadus, Andrus. *The Structure of Socialist Society*. New York: St. Martin's Press, 1977.

Hegel, George W. F. *The Philosophy of Mind*, trans. William Wallace. Oxford: Clarendon Press, 1894.

Henfrey, Colin. "Dependency, Modes of Production, and the Class Analysis of Latin America." *Latin American Perspectives* 30–31 (Summer, Fall 1981):17–54.

Hinton, William. *Fanshen: A Documentary of Revolution in a Chinese Village*. New York: Vintage Books, 1966.

Ho Ping-ti. *The Ladder of Success Imperial China*. New York: Columbia University Press, 1962.

Hoffman, Charles. *Work Incentive Practices and Policies in the People's Republic of China: 1953–1965*. Albany: State University of New York Press, 1967.

Horvat, Branko. *Towards a Theory of Planned Economy*. Belgrade: Yugoslav Institute of Economic Research, 1964.

Horvat, Branko, Mihailo Markovic, and Rudi Supek, eds. *Self-Governing Socialism: A Reader*, 2 vols. White Plains, N.Y.: International Arts and Sciences Press, 1975.

Hough, Jerry F. *The Soviet Union and Social Science Theory*. Cambridge: Harvard University Press, 1972.

Hsiao, Kung-chuan. *A History of Chinese Political Thought*, trans. F. W. Mote. Princeton: Princeton University Press, 1979.

Hsing Kuo-ch'iang. "Composition of the Eleventh CCPCC." *Issues and Studies* 10 (October 1977):13–60.

———. "Chinese Communist Cadre Problems." *Issues and Studies* 9 (September 1980):53–60.

Hsu, Kai-yu, ed. *Literature of the People's Republic of China*. Bloomington: Indiana University Press, 1980.

Hsuan Mo. "Bureaucratism in China: Its Causes." *Issues and Studies* 4 (April 1982):12–21.

Hsun-Tzu. *Basic Writings*. Trans. Burton Watson. New York: Columbia University Press, 1963.

Hua Guofeng. *Continue the Revolution under the Dictatorship of the Proletariat to the End*. Beijing: Foreign Languages Press, 1977.

———. "Report on the Work of Government." In *Documents of the First Session of the Fifth NPC*. Beijing: Foreign Languages Press, 1978.

Huang, Philip C. C., ed. *Development of Underdevelopment in China*. White Plains, N.Y.: M. E. Sharpe, 1980.

Institute for the Study of Chinese Communist Problems. *Collection of the Underground Mainland Publications*, 11 vols. Taipei, Taiwan: Shanghai Press, 1981.

Israel, Joachin. *Alienation: From Marx to Modern Sociology*. Boston: Allyn & Bacon, 1971.

Jenner, W. J. F. "1979: A New Start for Literature in China?" *China Quarterly* 86 (June 1981):274–303.

Jin Sheng (Wei Jingshen). "From the Walls of Peking: The Fifth Modernization." *Dissent* (Summer 1979):278–291.

Johnson, Chalmers, ed. *Ideology and Politics in Contemporary China*. Seattle: University of Washington Press, 1973.

Kan Tang. "Peiping's Anti-Bureaucracy Drive." *Issues and Studies* 4 (April 1982):22–36.

Kang Chao. "The China-Watchers Tested." *China Quarterly* 81 (March 1980):97–104.

King, Richard. " 'Wounds' and 'Exposure': Chinese Literature after the Gang of Four." *Pacific Affairs* 54 (Spring 1981):82–99.

Klatt, W. "Chinese Statistics Updated." *China Quarterly* 84 (December 1980):668–680.

Knight, Nick. "Mao Zedong's 'On Contradiction' and 'On Practice': Pre-liberation Texts." *China Quarterly* 84 (December 1980):641–680.

Kolakowski, Leszek. *Main Currents of Marxism*. Vol. 3: *The Breakdown*. Oxford: Clarendon Press, 1978.

Konrad, George and Ivan Szelenyi. *Intellectuals on the Road to Class Power*. New York: Harcourt Brace Jovanovich, 1979.

Korzec, Michel and Martin King Whyte. "Reading Notes: The Chinese Wage System." *China Quarterly* 86 (June 1981):243–273.

Kraus, Richard Curt. *Class Conflict in Chinese Socialism*. New York: Columbia University Press, 1981.

Krejci, Jaroslav. *Social Change and Stratification in Postwar Czechoslovakia*. New York: Columbia University Press, 1972.

Kuhn, Thomas S. *The Structure of Scientific Revolutions*, 2d ed. Chicago: University of Chicago Press, 1970.

Kung, Hans and Jürgen Moltmann. *Conflicting Ways of Interpreting the Bible*. New York: Seabury Press, 1980.

Kuusinen, O. V., ed. *Fundamentals of Marxism-Leninism*. Moscow: Foreign Languages Publishing House, 1962.

Lai Fung-wai. "Contradictions among Personal Status, Family Status and the Concept of Class in the People's Republic of China." Paper prepared for the Association of Asian Studies Conference, Gainesville, Florida, January 20–23, 1977.

Lande, Carl, ed. *Friends, Followers and Factions: A Reader in Political Clientelism*. Berkeley: University of California Press, 1977.

Landtman, Gunnar. *The Origin of the Inequality of the Social Classes*. Chicago: University of Chicago Press, 1938.

Lane, David. *The End of Inequality?* Baltimore, Md.: Penguin Books, 1971.

———. *The Socialist Industrial State*. Boulder: Westview Press, 1976.

Lao Tsu. "Tao Teh King." In *The Texts of Taoism*, trans. James Legge, 47–124. New York: Dover Publications, 1962.

Lardy, Nicholas R., ed. *Chinese Economic Planning: Translations of Chi-Hua Ching-Chi*. White Plains, N.Y.: M. E. Sharpe, 1977–1978.

———. *Economic Growth and Distribution in China*. Cambridge: Cambridge University Press, 1978.

———. "Recent Chinese Economic Performance and Prospects for the Ten-Year Plan." In *Chinese Economy Post-Mao*, U.S. Congress, Joint Economic Committee Print, 95th Congress, 2d sess., 48–62. Washington, D.C.: Government Printing Office, 1978.

———. "Living Standards and the Distribution of Income." Paper presented at the Conference on Development and Distribution in China, Centre of Asian Studies, University of Hong Kong, March 14–17, 1983.

Lee, Hong Yung. *The Politics of the Chinese Cultural Revolution*. Berkeley: University of California Press, 1978.

———. "The Politics of Cadre Rehabilitation since the Cultural Revolution." *Asian Survey* 18 (September 1978):934–955.

Lenin, Vladimir I. "A Great Beginning." Vol. 2: *Essentials of Lenin*, 490–495. London: Lawrence and Wishart, 1947.

———. *Collected Works*, 11 vols. Moscow: Progress Publishers, 1959–1966.

———. "What Is to Be Done? Burning Questions of Our Movement." In *Collected Works*, vol. 5, 347–529. Moscow: Progress Publishers, 1964.

———. *Economics and Politics in the Era of the Dictatorship of the Proletariat*. Moscow: Progress Publishers, 1978.

Lenski, Gerhard E. *Power and Privilege*. New York: McGraw-Hill, 1966.

Levada, Iu A. "Social Structure." In *Social Stratification and Mobility in the USSR*, ed. Murray Yanowitch and Wesley A. Fisher, 1–9. White Plains, N.Y.: International Arts and Sciences Press, 1973.

Levenson, Joseph R. *Modern China and Its Confucian Past*. Garden City, N.Y.: Doubleday, 1964.

———. *Confucian China and Its Modern Fate: A Trilogy*, 3 vols. Berkeley: University of California Press, 1965.

Lewis, John L., ed. *The City in Communist China*. Stanford: Stanford University Press, 1971.

Lewis, John W. *Leadership in Communist China*. Ithaca, N.Y.: Cornell University Press, 1963.

Leys, Simon. *Chinese Shadows*. New York: Viking Press, 1977.

Liang Chi-chao. *A History of Chinese Political Thought*. New York: Harcourt Brace and Co., 1930.

Lin Boye and Shen Zhe. "Commenting on the So-Called Opposition to the Class of Bureaucrats." *HQ* 5 (March 1981):17–26.

Lin Wei and Arnold V. Chao, eds. *China's Economic Reforms*. Philadelphia: University of Pennsylvania Press, 1982.

Liu Binyan. "Between Human and Demon." In *The New Realism: Writings from Chin after the Cultural Revolution*, ed. Lee Yee, 195–249. New York: Hippocrene Books, 1983.

Liu Shao-ch'i. *Collected Works of Liu Shao-ch'i*, 3 vols. Hong Kong: Union Research Institute, 1968–1969.

———. *Three Essays on Party Building*. Beijing: Foreign Languages Press, 1980.

Lowe, Donald M. *The Function of "China" in Marx, Lenin and Mao*. Berkeley: University of California Press, 1966.

Lu Xinhua, Liu Xinwu, eds. *The Wounded New Stories of the Cultural Revolution, 1977–1978*, trans. Geremie Barme and Bennett Lee. Hong Kong: Joint Publishing Co., 1979.

Lukacs, Georg. *History and Class Consciousness*, trans. Rodney Livingstone. Cambridge: MIT Press, 1971.

Lunacharsky, Anatoly. "Theses on the Problems of Marxist Literary Criticism," in *On Literature and Art*, A. Lebedev, comp. Moscow: Progress Publishers, 1973.

MacFarquhar, Roderick, ed. *The Hundred Flowers Campaign and the Chinese Intellectuals*. New York: Praeger Press, 1960.

McKnight, Brian C. "Fiscal Privileges and Social Order in Sung China," in *Crisis and Prosperity in Sung China*, ed. John Winthrop Haegar. Tucson: University of Arizona Press, 1975.

McLellan, David. *Marxism after Marx*. New York: Harper & Row, 1979.

McNaughton, William, ed. *The Confucian Vision*. Ann Arbor: University of Michigan Press, 1974.

Machetzki, Rudiger. "Provincial Income Differentials in China's Major Economic Development Area." Paper presented at the Conference on Development and Distribution in China, Centre of Asian Studies, University of Hong Kong, March 14–17, 1983.

Mandel, Arthur P., ed. *The Essential Works of Marxism*. New York: Bantam Books, 1961.

Marcuse, Herbert. *Soviet Marxism*. New York: Columbia University Press, 1958.

——. *One Dimensional Man*. Boston: Beacon Press, 1964.

Markovic, Mihailo. *From Affluence to Praxis*. Ann Arbor: University of Michigan Press, 1974.

———. "Socialism and Self-Management." In *Self-Governing Socialism*, vol. 1, ed. Branko Horvat, Mihailo Markovic, and Rudi Supek, 327–350. White Plains, N.Y.: International Arts and Sciences Press, 1975.

Markovic, Mihailo and Gado Petrovic, eds. *Praxis*. Boston: D. Reidel, 1979.

Marx, Karl. "The Eighteenth Brumaire of Louis Bonaparte." In Karl Marx and Frederick Engels, *Selected Works*, 1:394–487. Moscow: Progress Publishers, 1969.

———. *Grundrisse*, trans. Martin Nicolaus. New York: Vintage Books, 1973.

———. "Economic and Philosophical Manuscripts" (1844). In *Early Writings*, trans. Rodney Livingstone, 279–400. New York: Vintage Books, 1975.

———. *Capital*, 3 vols. trans. David Fernback. New York: Vintage Books, 1981.

Marx, Karl and Frederick Engels. *Selected Works*, 3 vols. Moscow: Progress Publishers, 1969–1970.

———. "Feuerbach: Opposition of the Materialistic and Idealistic Outlook." In *Selected Works*, 1:16–80. Moscow: Progress Publishers, 1969.

———. "Marx's Letter to Weydemeyer." In *Selected Works*, 1:528. Moscow: Progress Publishers, 1969.

Mathews, Mervyn. *Class and Society in Soviet Russia*. London: Penguin Press, 1972.

———. *Privilege in the Soviet Union*. London: Allen & Unwin, 1978.

Maxwell, Neville, ed. *China's Road to Development*, 2d ed. New York: Pergamon Press, 1979.

Meisner, Maurice. "Utopian Goals and Ascetic Values in Chinese Communist Ideology." *Journal of Asian Studies* 1 (November 1968):101–110.

———. *Mao's China: A History of the People's Republic*. New York: Free Press, 1977.

———. *Li Ta-chao and the Origin of Chinese Marxism*. New York: Atheneum Press, 1979.

Mesa-Lago, Carmelo and Carl Beck, eds. *Comparative Socialist Systems*. Pittsburgh: University of Pittsburgh Press, 1975.

Miliband, Ralph. *The State in Capitalist Society*. London: Weidenfeld and Nicholson, 1969.

Mills, C. Wright, ed. *The Marxists*. New York: Dell Publishing, 1962.

Mokrosonov, G. V. "On the Criteria of Interclass Differences in Socialist Society." In *Social Stratification and Mobility in the USSR*, ed. Murray Yanowitch and Wesley A. Fisher, 122–126. White Plains, N.Y.: International Arts and Sciences Press, 1973.

Moore, Barrington. *Social Origins of Dictatorship and Democracy*. Boston: Beacon Press, 1966.

———. *Injustice: The Social Basis of Obedience and Revolt*. White Plains, N.Y.: M. E. Sharpe, 1978.

"More on the Historical Experience of the Dictatorship of the Proletariat." *RMRB* (December 19, 1956). In *Readings in Chinese Communist Documents*, ed. Wen-shun Chi, 127–156. Berkeley: University of California Press, 1968.

Morris, Monica B. *An Excursion into Creative Sociology*. New York: Columbia University Press, 1977.

Mosca, Gaetano. *The Ruling Class*. New York: McGraw-Hill, 1939.

Munro, Donald J. *The Concept of Man in Early China*. Stanford: Stanford University Press, 1969.

———. "The Chinese View of 'Alienation.' " *China Quarterly* 59 (July-September 1974):580–582.

———. *The Concept of Man in Contemporary China*. Ann Arbor: University of Michigan Press, 1977.

Muravchik, Joshua. "Theories of the New Class." *World Affairs* 2 (Fall 1981):105–191.

Needham, Joseph. *Science and Civilization in China*, vol. 2. Cambridge: Cambridge University Press, 1962.

Oleszczuk, Thomas. "Dissident Marxism in Eastern Europe." *World Politics* 4 (July 1982):527–547.

Orleans, Leo A. "Soviet Perceptions of China's Economic Development." In *Chinese Economy Post-Mao*, U.S. Congress. Joint Economic Committee Print, 95th Congress, 2d sess., 155–164. Washington, D.C.: Government Printing Office, 1978.

Ossowski, Stanislaw. "Old Notions and New Problems: Interpretations of Social Structure in Modern Society." In *Translations of the Third World Congress of Sociology*, vol. 3, 18–25. London: International Sociological Association, 1956.

———. *Class Structure in the Social Consciousness*. New York: Free Press, 1963.

Palmer, Richard E. *Hermeneutics: Interpretation Theory in Schleiermacher, Dilthey, Heidegger and Gadamer*. Evanston: Northwestern University Press, 1969.

Parkin, Frank. *Class, Inequality and Political Order*. New York: Praeger Publishers, 1971.

———., ed. *The Social Analysis of Class Structure*. London: Tavistock Publishers, 1974.

———. *Marxism and Class Theory: A Bourgeois Critique*. New York: Columbia University Press, 1979.

Parrish, William L. and Martin K. Whyte. *Village and Family Life in Contemporary China*. Chicago: University of Chicago Press, 1978.

Parsons, Talcott. *The Structure of Social Action*. New York: McGraw-Hill, 1948.

Pasic, Najdan. "The Idea of Direct Self-Managing Democracy and Socialization of Policy-Making." In *Self-Governing Socialism*, vol. 1, ed. Branko Horvat, Mihailo Markovic, and Rudi Supek, 34–40. White Plains, N.Y.: International Arts and Sciences Press, 1975.

Pepper, Suzanne. "Education and Revolution: The 'Chinese Model' Revisited." *Asian Survey* 18 (September 1978):847–890.

———. *China's Universities*. Michigan Papers No. 46. Ann Arbor: University of Michigan Press, 1984.

Perkins, Dwight H. *Market Control and Planning in Communist China*. Cambridge: Harvard University Press, 1966.

Pervan, Ralph. "Yugoslavia: Toward Self-Management." In *The Withering Away of the State?* ed. Leslie Holmes, 223–244. London: Sage Publications, 1981.

Peterson, Albert S. "China: Transportation Developments, 1971–1980." In *China under the Four Modernizations*, pt. 1, U.S. Congress, Joint Economic Committee. Joint Committee Print, 97th Congress, 2d sess., 138–170. Washington, D.C.: Government Printing Office, 1982.

Pfeffer, Richard M. "Mao and Marx in the Marxist-Leninist Tradition." *Modern China* 4 (October 1976):421–460.

———. "Mao and Marx: Understanding Scholarship and Ideology—A Response." *Modern China* 4 (October 1977):380–382.

Plato. "The Republic." In *Great Dialogues of Plato*, trans. W. H. D. Rouse, 118–422. New York: Mentor Books, 1956.

Poulantzas, Nicos. *Political Power and Social Classes*. London: New Left Books, 1973.

———. *State, Power, Socialism*. London: New Left Books, 1978.

Prybyla, Jan S. *Issues in Socialist Economic Modernization*. New York: Praeger, 1980.

———. *The Chinese Economy: Problems and Policies*, 2d ed. Columbia: University of South Carolina Press, 1981.

———. "Key Issues in the Chinese Economy." *Asian Survey* 21 (September 1981):925–946.

Pye, Lucian W. *The Dynamics of Factions and Consensus in Chinese Politics*. Santa Monica: Rand Corporation, 1980.

Rabinow, Paul and William M. Sullivan, eds. *Interpretive Social Science: A Reader*. Berkeley: University of California Press, 1979.

Rawski, Thomas G. *Economic Growth and Employment in China*. New York: Oxford University Press, 1979.

———. *China's Transition to Industrialism*. Ann Arbor: University of Michigan Press, 1980.

"Revolutionary Literature in China." *Bulletin of Concerned Asian Scholars* 8:1, 2 (1976).

Reynolds, Bruce L. "Reform in Industrial Management: An Empirical Report." In *China under the Four Modernizations*, pt. 1, U.S. Congress, Joint Economic Committee, Joint Committee Print, 97th Congress, 2d sess., 119–137. Washington, D.C.: Government Printing Office, 1982.

Richman, Barry. *Industrial Society in Communist China*. New York: Random House, 1969.

Ricoeur, Paul. *The Conflict of Interpretations: Essays in Hermeneutics*. Evanston: Northwestern University Press, 1974.

———. *Freud and Philosophy: An Essay on Interpretation*, trans. Dennis Savage. New Haven: Yale University Press, 1978.

———. "The Model of the Text: Meaningful Action Considered as Text." In *Interpretive Social Science: A Reader*, ed. Paul Rabinow and William N. Sullivan, 13–102. Berkeley: University of California Press, 1979.

Rigby, T. H. and Ferenc Feher. *Political Legitimation in Communist States*. New York: St. Martin's Press, 1982.

Roberts, Paul Craig. *Alienation and the Soviet Economy*. Albuquerque: University of New Mexico Press, 1971.

Runciman, W. G. "Towards a Theory of Social Stratification." In *The Social Analysis of Class Structure*, ed. Frank Parkin, 55–101. London: Tavistock Publishers, 1974.

Rutkevich, M. N. and F. R. Filippov. "Principles of the Marxist Approach to Social Stratification and Social Mobility." In *Social Stratification and Mobility in the USSR*, ed. Murray Yanowitch and Wesley A. Fisher, 229–240. White Plains, N.Y.: International Arts and Sciences Press, 1973.

Scalapino, Robert D., ed. *Elites in the People's Republic of China*. Seattle: University of Washington Press, 1972.

Schillebeeckx, Edward. *Jesus: An Experiment in Christology*, trans. Huber Hoskins. New York: Vintage Books, 1981.

Schoppa, R. Keith. *Chinese Elites and Political Change*. Cambridge: Harvard University Press, 1982.

Schram, Stuart R. *The Political Thought of Mao Tse-tung*. New York: Praeger, 1963.

———. "Mao Tse-tung and the Theory of the Permanent Revolution." *China Quarterly* 46 (April-June 1971):221–244.

———. "To Utopia and Back: A Cycle in the History of the CCP." *China Quarterly* 87 (September 1981):407–439.

Schurmann, Franz. *Ideology and Organization in Communist China*, 2d ed. Berkeley: University of California Press, 1968.

Schwartz, Benjamin I. *Chinese Communism and the Rise of Mao*. Cambridge: Harvard University Press, 1951.

———. *Communism and China: Ideology in Flux*. Cambridge: Harvard University Press, 1968.

———. "The Essence of Marxism Revisited." *Modern China* 4 (October 1976):461–472.

Scott, James C. *The Moral Economy of the Peasant*. New Haven: Yale University Press, 1976.

Selden, Mark. *The Yenan Way in Revolutionary China*. Cambridge: Harvard University Press, 1971.

Senese, Donald J. "Adam Smith versus Karl Marx in China." *Journal of Social and Political Economic Studies* (Fall 1985):277–304.

Shapiro, Michael J. *Language and Political Understanding: The Politics of Discursive Practices*. New Haven: Yale University Press, 1981.

Sherman, Howard. *Radical Political Economy*. New York: Basic Books, 1972.

Shirk, Susan L. "Recent Chinese Labour Policies and the Transformation of Industrial Organization in China." *China Quarterly* 88 (December 1981):573–593.

Shkaratan, O. I. "Social Groups in the Working Class of a Developed Socialist Society." In *Social Stratification and Mobility in the USSR*, trans. and ed. Murray Yanowitch and Wesley A. Fisher, 79–100. White Plains, N.Y.: International Arts and Sciences Press, 1973.

———. "Sources of Social Differentiation of the Working Class in Soviet Society." In *Social Stratification and Mobility in the USSR*, trans. and ed. Murray Yanowitch and Wesley A. Fisher, 10–21. White Plains, N.Y.: International Arts and Sciences Press, 1973.

Singer, Daniel. "Class Struggles in Poland: Notes on a Historic Compromise." *Monthly Review* 6 (November 1980):14–29.

Skocpol, Theda. *States and Social Revolutions*. Cambridge: Harvard University Press, 1979.

Smith, Hedrick. *The Russians*. New York: Quadrangle Books, 1976.

Snow, Edgar. *Red Star over China*. New York: Random House, 1938.

———. *The Long Revolution*. New York: Random House, 1972.

Solinger, Dorothy S. "Economic Reform via Reformulation in China: Where Do Rightist Ideas Come From?" *Asian Survey* 9 (September 1981):947–960.

Solomon, Richard H. *Mao's Revolution and the Chinese Political Culture*. Berkeley: University of California Press, 1971.

Staal, Frits. "Oriental Ideas on the Origin of Language." *Journal of the American Oriental Society* 1 (January-March 1979):1–14.

Stalin, Joseph. *Dialectical and Historical Materialism*. New York: International Publishers, 1977.

Stark, David. "Class Struggle and the Transformation of the Labor Process." *Theory and Society* 9 (January 1980):89–130.

Starr, John Bryan. "Mao's Self-Image." *Modern China* 4 (October 1977):435–442.

———. *Continuing the Revolution: The Political Thought of Mao*. Princeton: Princeton University Press, 1979.

Stinchcombe, Arthur L. *Constructing Social Theories*. New York: Harcourt Brace and World, 1968.

Stojanovic, Svetozar. *Between Ideals and Reality*. London: Oxford University Press, 1973.

———. "A Tension in Historical Materialism." In *Praxis*, ed. Mihailo Markovic and Gado Petrovic, 63–79. Boston: D. Reidel, 1979.

Strauss, Leo. *What Is Political Philosophy?* New York: Free Press, 1959.

———. *The City and Man*. Chicago: Rand McNally, 1964.

Suchting, W. "Knowledge and Practice: Towards a Marxist Critique of Traditional Epistemology." *Science and Society* 47 (Spring 1983):1–13.

Sweezy, Paul M. and Charles Bettelheim. *On the Transition to Socialism*. New York: Monthly Review Press, 1971.

———. "Post-Revolutionary Society." *Monthly Review* 6 (November 1980):1–21.

Tan, Chester C. *Chinese Political Thought in the Twentieth Century*. New York: Doubleday and Co., 1971.

T'ang Chun-I. "The Individual and the World in Chinese Methodology." In *The Status of the Individual in East and West*, ed. Charles A. Moore, 101–119. Honolulu: University of Hawaii Press, 1968.

Taubman, Wolfgang. "Problems of Urban Housing in the People's Republic of China." Paper presented at the Conference on Development and Distribution in China, Centre of Asian Studies, University of Hong Kong, March 14–17, 1983.

Tawney, R. H. *Equality*. London: Allen & Unwin, 1931.

———. *Land and Labor in China*. New York: Harcourt Brace and Co., 1932.

Taylor, John G. *From Modernization to Modes of Production*. Atlantic Highlands, N.J.: Humanities Press, 1979.

Thompson, E. P. *The Poverty of Theory and Other Essays*. London: Monthly Review Press, 1978.

Tiewes, Frederick C. *Elite Discipline in China*. Canberra: Contemporary China Center, Australian National University, 1978.

———. *Politics and Purges in China*. White Plains, N.Y.: M. E. Sharpe, 1979.

Townsend, James. *Political Participation in Communist China*. Berkeley: University of California Press, 1967.

Triska, Jan and Paul M. Cocks. *Political Development in East Europe*. New York: Praeger Publishers, 1977.

Trotsky, Leon. *The Revolution Betrayed*. New York: Pioneer Publishers, 1945.

———. *Literature and Revolution*. Ann Arbor: University of Michigan Press, 1960.

Tsou, Tang, Marc Blecher, and Mitch Meisner. "The Responsibility System in Agriculture: Its Implementation by Xiyang and Dazhai." *Modern China* 8 (January 1982):41–103.

Tucker, Robert C. *The Marxian Revolutionary Idea*. New York: W. W. Norton, 1969.

———. *Philosophy and Myth in Karl Marx*. London: Cambridge University Press, 1972.

Tung, Rosalie L. *Chinese Industrial Society after Mao*. Lexington, Mass.: D. C. Heath, 1982.

Twelfth National Congress of the CPC (September 1982). Beijing: Foreign Languages Press, 1982.

U.S. Congress, Joint Economic Committee. *Chinese Economy Post-Mao*. Joint Committee Print, 95th Congress, 2d sess. Washington, D.C.: Government Printing Office, 1978.

———. *China under the Four Modernizations*, pt. 1. Joint Committee Print, 97th Congress, 2d sess. Washington, D.C.: Government Printing Office, 1982.

Vermeer, Edward B. "Social Welfare Provisions and the Limits of Inequality in Contemporary China." *Asian Survey* 9 (September 1979):856–880.

Wakeman, Frederick, Jr. *History and Will: Philosophical Perspectives of Mao Tse-tung's Thought*. Berkeley: University of California Press, 1973.

Walder, Andrew G. "Marxism, Maoism, and Social Change." *Modern China* 2 (April 1977):101–118, 125–160.

Wang Hsiao-hsien. "Wage Adjustments in Communist China." *Issues and Studies* 2 (February 1978):12–21.

Wang Meng. "A New Young Man Arrives at the Organization Department." *Current Background* No. 459, pp. 1–32. Hong Kong: American Consulate, June 28, 1957.

Wang Xizhe. "For a Return to Genuine Marxism in China." *New Left Review* 121 (May-June 1980):33–48.

Webb, Eugene, Donald Campbell, et al. *Unobtrusive Measures: Non-Reactive Research in the Social Sciences*. Chicago: Rand McNally, 1966.

Weber, Max. *The Theory of Social and Economic Organization*, ed. Talcott Parsons. New York: Oxford University Press, 1947.

———. "Bureaucracy." In *Images of Man*, ed. C. Wright Mills, 149–192. New York: George Braziller, 1960.

White, Gordon. *The Politics of Class and Class Origin: The Case of the Cultural Revolution*. Canberra: Contemporary China Centre, Australian National University, 1976.

White, Stephen, John Gardner, and George Schopflin, eds. *Communist Political Systems: An Introduction*. New York: St. Martin's Press, 1982.

Whyte, Martin King. *Small Groups and Political Rituals in China*. Berkeley: University of California Press, 1974.

———. "Inequality and Stratification in China." *China Quarterly* 64 (October 1975):684–711.

Widor, Claude, ed. *Documents sur le mouvement democratique chinois: 1978–1980*, vol. 1. Paris: Editions de l'École des hautes études en sciences sociales, 1981.

Wilhelm, Richard. *The I-Ching: Or Book of Changes*, trans. Cary F. Baynes, 3d ed. Princeton: Princeton University Press, 1967.

Wittfogel, Karl A. *Oriental Despotism*. New Haven: Yale University Press, 1957.

Wong, Paul. *China's Higher Leadership in the Socialist Transition*. London: Free Press, 1976.

Wood, George Herbert. *Christianity and Communism*. New York: Round Table Press, 1933.

Wortzel, Larry M. "Incentive Mechanisms and Remuneration in China: Policies of the Eleventh Central Committee." *Asian Survey* 21 (September 1981):961–976.

Wright, Arthur F. and Dennis Twitchett, eds. *Confucian Personalities*. Stanford: Stanford University Press, 1962.

Wright, Erik Olin. *Class, Crisis and the State*. London: New Left Books, 1978.

———. "Class and Occupation." *Theory and Society* 9 (January 1980):177–214.

Xiao Liang. "Changing the Leadership System in State Enterprises." In *China's Economic Reforms*, ed. Lin Wei and Arnold Chao, 147–158. Philadelphia: University of Pennsylvania Press, 1982.

Xue Muqiao. *China's Socialist Economy*. Beijing: Foreign Languages Press, 1981.

———. *Current Economic Problems in China*, ed., trans. and intro. K. K. Fung. Boulder, Colo.: Westview Press, 1982.

Yang, C. K. *A Chinese Village in Early Communist Transition*, 2 vols. Cambridge: MIT Press, 1959.

Yang I-fan. *The Case Against Hu Feng*. Hong Kong: Union Research Institute, 1956.

Yanowitch, Murray. *Social and Economic Inequality in the Soviet Union*. White Plains, N.Y.: M. E. Sharpe, 1977.

Yao Wen-yuan. *On the Social Basis of the Lin Piao Anti-Party Clique*. Beijing: Foreign Languages Press, 1975.

Ye Jianying. *Speech at the Meeting in Celebration of the 30th Anniversary of the Founding of the People's Republic of China* (September 19, 1979). Beijing: Foreign Languages Press, 1979.

Yee, Lee, ed. *The New Realism: Writings from China after the Cultural Revolution*. New York: Hippocrene Books, 1983.

Young, Graham and Dennis Woodward. "From Contradictions among the People to Class Struggle: The Theories of Uninterrupted Revolution and Continuous Revolution." *Asian Survey* 9 (September 1978):912–933.

MAO ZEDONG'S WRITINGS

Selected Works of Mao Tse-tung, 4 vols. Beijing: Foreign Languages Press, 1975.

Selected Works of Mao Tse-tung, Vol. 5. Beijing: Foreign Languages Press, 1977. [Hereafter all five volumes cited as *SW*.]

"Analysis of Classes in Chinese Society." *SW*, 1:13–22.

"On Contradiction." *SW*, 1:311–345.

"On the Correct Handling of Contradictions among the People." *SW*, 5:384–421.

"How to Differentiate the Classes in Rural Areas." *SW*, 1:137–140.

"On New Democracy." *SW*, 2:339–384.

"On the People's Democratic Dictatorship." *SW*, 4:411–424.

"On Practice." *SW*, 1:295–310.

"On Production by the Army for Its Own Support and on the Great Movements for Rectification and for Production." *SW*, 2:275–279.

"On the Question of the National Bourgeoisic and the Enlightened Gentry." *SW*, 4:207–210.

"Rectify the Party's Style of Work." *SW*, 3:35–51.

"Report on the Investigation of the Peasant Movement in Hunan." *SW*, 1:23–59.

"The Role of the Chinese Communist Party in the National War." *SW*, 2:195–211.

"Sixty Points on Working Methods—A Draft Resolution from the Office of the Center of the CCP'' (February 19, 1958). In *Mao's Papers*, ed. Jerome Ch'en, 57–76. London: Oxford University Press, 1970.

''Some Questions Concerning Methods of Leadership.'' *SW*, 2:117–122.

''On the Ten Major Relationships.'' *SW*, 5:267–288.

''Talks at the Yanan Forum on Literature and Art.'' *SW*, 3:69–98.

''The Tasks of the Chinese Communist Party in the Period of Resistance to Japan.'' *SW*, 1:263–283.

''Twenty Manifestations of Bureaucracy.'' JPRS 49826 (February 12, 1970).

CHINESE LANGUAGE EDUCATIONAL MATERIALS

Beijing daxue. *Zhongguo zhexueshi*, 2 vols. Beijing: Zhonghua shuju, 1980.

———. *Zhongguo zhexueshi jiaoxue ziliao xuanji*, 2 vols. Beijing: Zhonghua shuju, 1980.

———. *Xifang zhexue yuanzhu xuandu*, 2 vols. Beijing: Shangwu yinshuguan, 1982.

Jingji yanjiu bianjibu. *Shehui zhuji zhengzhi jingjixue rougan jiben lilun wenti*. Jinan: Shandong chubanshe, 1980.

Li Honglin. *Kexue he mixin*. Tianjin: Renmin chubanshe, 1980.

Nanfang shiliusuo daxue. *Zhengzhi Jingjixue*, 2 vols. Shanghai: Shanghai renmin chubanshe, 1978.

Shanghaishi laodongju, ed. *Jianguo yilai anlao fenpeilun wenxuan*, 2 vols. Shanghai: Shanghai renmin chubanshe, 1978.

Sun Shangqing. ''Duiyu woguo jingji jiegou wenti de chubu yanjiu.'' In Shehui zhuyi zhengzhi jingjixue ruogan jiben lilun wenti, Jingji yanjiu bianjibu, 17–36. Jinan: Shandong chubanshe, 1980.

Sun Yuefang. *Shehui zhuyi jingji di rougan lilun wenti*. Wuhan: Renmin chubanshe, 1982.

Wan Bin. *Lun shehuizhuyi ziyou*. Beijing: Qunzhong chubanshe, 1982.

Wu Jiang. *Renshilun shijiang*. Shanghai: Shanghai renmin chubanshe, 1981.

———. *Guanyu yanjiu Mao Zedong zhexue sixiang di jige wenti*. Beijing: Beijing chubanshe, 1982.

Zhexue yicong bianjibu. *Jin xiandai xifang zhuyao zhexue liupai ziliao*. Beijing: Shangwu yinshuguan, 1982.

Zhongguo renmin daxue. *Zhonggou jindai jingjishi*, 2 vols. Beijing: Renmin chubanshe, 1976.

Zhongguo shehui kexueyuan qingbao yanjiusuo. *Sulian lilun jielun shehui zhuyi shehui di jieji*. Beijing: Zhonggou shehui kexueyuan chubanshe, 1980. (Nei Bu)

Zhunze xuexi fudao. *Guanyu dangnei zhengzhi shenghuo de ruogan zhunze*. Zhenjiang: Jiangsu renmin chubanshe, 1980.

Zhongguo zhengzhi xuehui. *Zhengzhi yu zhengzhi kexue*. Beijing: Qunzhong chubanshe, 1981.

CHINESE LANGUAGE GENERAL SOURCES

Ai Hengrui and Lin Qingshan. "Yi fen wei er" yu "he er er yi." *GMRB*, May 29, 1964.

Chongfang de xianhua. Shanghai: Wenyi chubanshe, 1979.

Deng Xiaoping. *Deng Xiaoping tongzhi tanduan zhengdangfeng wenti*. Jiangxi: Hongqi chubanshe, 1981.

Du Shuying and Li Zhongyue. "Dangxing yuanze yu yishu guilu." *WXPL* (May 1981):76–79.

Fu Suilan. "Du: Zhongguo shehui ge jieji de fenxi."*Xin jianshe* (February 1952):19–21.

Gong-sun Long. "Bai ma lun." In *Zhongguo zhexueshi jiaoxue ziliao xuanji*, ed. Beijing daxue zhexuexi zhongguo zhexueshi jiaoyanshi xuanju, 182–185. Beijing: Zhonghua shuzhu, 1981.

Guanyu dangnei zhengzhi shenghuo de ruogan zhunze (Beijing: Renmin chubanshe, 1980).

Guo Yongxian, Xue Hanwei, Pan Guohua. "Ma Ke Si zhuyi yu jieji douzheng." *RMRB*, February 1, 1980.

Li Xiulin and Zheng Hangsheng. "Meiyou boxue jieji de jieji douzheng." *RMRB*, October 31, 1979.

Li Yizhe. "Guanyu shehui zhuyi de minzhu yu fazhi." In *Minzhu zhonghua*, ed. Xianggang zhongwen daxue, 53–82. Hong Kong: Zhongwen daxue xueshenghui, 1982.

Liu Qing. *Yuzhong shouji*. Hong Kong: Baixing chubanshe, 1981.

Ma ke Se. *Jingjixue—Zhexue shougao*. trans. He Sijing. Beijing: Renmin chubanshe, 1963.

Minzhu zhonghua. Hong Kong: Zhongwen daxue xueshenghui, 1982.

Paobing zhishu jiguan wuchan jieji gemingpai. "Niannian buwang jieji douzheng, zhudong di chijiu di xiang jieji diren jingong." *RMRB*, April 23, 1968.

"Shijian shi jiancha zhenli de weiyi biaozhun." *RMRB*, May 12, 1978.

Wang Guixiu and Zhang Xianyang. "Dangqian jieji douzheng di duixiang shi shenme?" *RMRB*, October 31, 1979.

———. "Woguo xianjieduan di jieji douzheng he renmin neibu Maodun." *GMRB*, November 7, 1979.

Wang Xizhe. "Dang de lingdao yu minzhu jiandu." In *Minzhu zhonghua*, 310–318. Hong Kong: Xianggang zhongwen daxue xueshenghui, 1983.

Wang Zhengping. "Jieji jin jin shi yige jingji fanchou ma?" *RMRB*, January 4, 1980.

Wei Jingsheng. "Di Wuge xiandaihua—minzhu yu chita." In *Minzhu Zhonghua*, 167–191. Hong Kong: Zhongwen daxue xueshenghui, 1982.

Wen Hua. "Dangqian wenyi chuangzuo xuyao zhuyi de jige wenti." *HQ* 7 (November 7, 1982):29–31.

Xiao Wu. "Xuexi jieji fenxi fangfa." Xin Jianshe (February 1952):16–19.

Xu Dixin, "Lun woguo guomin jingji de biange yu fazhan." In *Shehuizhuyi zhengzhi jingjixue ruogan jiben lilun wenti*. Jinan: Shandong chubanshe, 1980.

Xu Xuejian. "Zhongguo de shedui qiye yu cheng-xiang fazhan." Paper presented at the Conference on Development and Distribution in China, Centre of Asian Studies, University of Hong Kong, March 14–17, 1983.

"Xuexi jieji zhuangkuang lunshu jiekaile san gen shengsuo." *RMRB*, April 27, 1979.

Yu Yannan. "Guanyu woguo zichan jieji zuowei boxue jieji xiaomie yihou de gongren jieji." *HQ* 16 (August 16, 1982):14–18.

1981 duanpian xiaoshuo xuan. Beijing: Renmin wenxue chubanshe, 1982.

Zhang Chao. "Yishu shilun." *WXPL* (June 1981):3–17.

Zhao Ziyang. "Guanyu dangqian jingji gongzuo de jige wenti." In 1982 *Zhongguo jingji nianjian*, pp. II-32–II-40. Beijing: Jingji guanli zazhi chubanshe, 1982.

Zhongguo gongchandang Shandong sheng weiyuanhui. "Jianchi jieji fenxi fangfa zhengque renshe luxian douzheng." *HQ* 13 (December 4, 1971):20–24.

Zhongguo jingji nianjian. 1981. Beijing: Jingji guanli zazhishe, 1981.

———. *1982*. Beijing: Jingji guanli zazhishe, 1982.

———. *1984*. Beijing: Jingji guanli zazhishe, 1984.

Zhongguo minzhu yundong ziliaoce. Hong Kong: Zhongwen daxue Xueshenghui (undated, obtained March 1983).

RENMIN WENXUE

Bai Hua. "Yi shu xinzha." *RMWX* 1 (January 1980):24–40.

Jiang Zilong. "Jidian juzhang de yi tian." *RMWX* 1 (January 1976):45–61.

———. "Tie xian zhuan." *RMWX* 4 (April 1976):39–55.

———. "Yige gongchang mixhu de riji." In *1980 Nian quan guo youxiu duanpian xiaoshuo pingxuan*, pp. 169–196. Shanghai: Shanghai wenyi chubanshe, 1981.

Jiao Zuyao. "Zhao huan." *RMWX* 7 (July 1980):81–86.

Li Zhun. "Da nian chuyi." *RMWX* 5 (May 1981):62–68.

Liu Wu. "Tongzhi." *RMWX* 2 (February 1978):85–89.

Qin Yanshen. " 'Tiao' duizhang jishi." *RMWX* 1 (January 1978):85–89.

Ru Zhijuan. "Jianji cuole di gushi." *RMWX* (February 1979):65–76.

Xu Huaizhong. "Xixian yishi." *RMWX* 1 (January 1980):3–23.

Ye Wenling. "Nianfan." *RMWX* 11 (November 1977):55–62.

Zhou Yongnian. "Zhuren." *RMWX* 3 (March 1976):32–41.

DISSIDENT LITERATURE

"Translations from Beijing Unofficial Journals." U.S. Joint Publications Research Service (JPRS) 33215 (April 12, 1979), JPRS 33421 (May 10, 1979), JPRS 73778 (June 20, 1979), JPRS 73756 (June 26, 1979), JPRS 73987 (August 9, 1979), JPRS 74591 (November 16, 1979).

Beijing zhiqun. (January-October 1979).

Minzhu qiang. (December 1978).

Qimeng. (January 1979).

Renmin luntan. (January 1979).

Siwu luntan. (December 1978-February 1979).

Tan Suo. 1 (January 8, 1979), 2 (January 29, 1979), 3 (March 4, 1979), 4 (September 9, 1979), 5 (October 1, 1979).

Zhongguo renquan. (January-February 1979).

Index

About the Author

LARRY M. WORTZEL, a Major in the United States Army, earned his Ph.D. in Political Science from the University of Hawaii. He serves as a Staff Assistant on International Security and Foreign Disclosure for the Office of the Under Secretary of Defense for Policy, where he helps to develop policy and establish national security programs. Major Wortzel has served in Korea, Thailand, and Singapore, and has traveled in Vietnam and extensively in China. He has published articles in *Asian Survey,* and is currently at work on a book analyzing the international implications of China's military modernization program.